The Official
DRIVER THEORY TEST
Questions and Answers

Published by Prometric Ireland Limited under licence from the Road Safety Authority.

© 2011 Údarás Um Shábháilteacht Ar Bhóithre / Road Safety Authority

5th edition, September 2011

ISBN 978-0-9570159-0-6

Prometric Ireland Limited
Grand Mill Quay
Barrow Street
Dublin 4
Ireland

Foreword

As a learner driver, it is important that you have all the information you need to drive safely on our roads. Before you drive on a public road or in a public place you must have a learner permit or a driving licence for the vehicle you want to drive. In most cases you must also pass a driver theory test to show that you understand what you must do to drive safely. The questions in the test, which are all in this book, are designed to test your knowledge and also to make you think about the different situations you will come across as a driver. By studying the learning material and passing the test you will have taken an important first step to becoming a safe driver. It is essential that you then apply your knowledge when you are on the road.

Learning to drive needs time and patience, and the best way to learn is to take driving lessons while practising as much as you can with an experienced driver. Learners taking out a first learner permit for a car must take the Essential Driver Training (EDT) programme, and learners taking out a learner permit for a motorcycle must take Initial Basic Training (IBT) – for more information, see www.rsa.ie. It is important to find an Approved Driving Instructor (ADI) that you are comfortable with and to listen carefully to the advice you get. Ask for help if you aren't sure of something and look up your copy of the Rules of the Road for guidance.

Finally, remember that driving should be enjoyable, and we wish you many years of safe driving.

Introduction

To drive a motor vehicle on the public road in Ireland, you must hold a driving licence or a learner permit that covers the particular category of vehicle you plan to drive. For licensing purposes, there are fourteen categories of vehicle, identified by code letters – for example a motorcar is category B, a moped is category M.

⊙ To obtain a learner permit, you must pass a driver theory test – that is what this book is about.

⊙ To obtain a full driving licence, you must first hold a learner permit, and you must pass a practical driving test.

With a learner permit, a number of restrictions apply, the most important of which is that you must be accompanied at all times by the holder of a full driving licence.

Who must take the driver theory test?

Before you can apply for your first learner permit in any category, you must have passed a driver theory test that relates to that category, and you must submit the driver theory test certificate to the licensing authority within two years of passing the test.

There are four different driver theory tests; which one you take depends on the category of vehicle you are planning to drive. This book covers all four tests, and different parts of the book are relevant to different tests, as shown below.

Category of vehicle you intend to drive		Theory test	Parts of this book from which questions will be taken for the test
B	Car and light van	BW	Parts 1 and 2
EB	Car and light van with trailer		
W	Tractor and works vehicle		
A	Motorcycle	AM	Parts 1 and 3
A1	Small motorcycle		
M	Moped		
C	Truck	C	Parts 1, 4 and 5
EC	Truck with trailer		
C1	Small truck		
EC1	Small truck with trailer		
D	Bus	D	Parts 1, 4 and 6
ED	Bus with trailer		
D1	Minibus		
ED1	Minibus with trailer		

Note that you do not have to pass the same theory test more than once. For example, if you pass the theory test for category C and obtain a learner permit for category C1, and you subsequently wish to obtain a learner permit for category C, you are not required to take another driver theory test, provided you still have a valid learner permit or driving licence for category C1.

Preparing for the driver theory test

You should use this book and/or the Driver Theory Test CD-ROM as well as the Rules of the Road to prepare for the driver theory test. This book contains the actual questions that will be asked in your driver theory test, along with the correct answer and a brief explanation.

If you spend sufficient time and effort preparing for your test, you should not find it difficult, and you should pass. More importantly, the knowledge you gain in preparing for the test will help to make you a better and a safer driver.

About the questions and answers in this book

In the test, you will be asked 40 questions, and to pass you must answer at least 35 correctly. The questions will be taken from those set out in this book – you will not get a question that is not in the book.

In the test, each question you are asked is accompanied by four possible answers. Only one of these answers is correct, and you are required to identify it. The test is computerised and you will get a chance to practice before the test, so that you are familiar with the format.

Applying for a driver theory test

When you feel that you are well-enough prepared, apply to the Driver Theory Testing Service in one of the following ways:

Online:	www.theorytest.ie.
By telephone:	For an English language test call: 1890 606 106 For an Irish language test call: 1890 606 806 To book a test by text phone call: 1890 616 216 (These telephone numbers are all LoCall numbers.)
By post:	Complete an application form (obtainable from any Motor Taxation Office or online from: www.theorytest.ie) and post it to: The Driver Theory Testing Service, PO Box 788 Togher, Cork. When applying, please specify any special needs or language requirements that you have, so that appropriate arrangements may be made.

When booking a test, please have to hand credit/debit card details and your PPS number (formally RSI number).

Information on where and when theory tests may be taken can be obtained by contacting the Driver Theory Testing Service as above.

Contents

Part 2: Cars, light vans, tractors and works vehicles 189

Part 4: Trucks and buses..............267

Part 5: Trucks only 301

Part 6: Buses only 321

Part 1

All vehicle categories

Road signs, markings and traffic regulations

As you drive along any road you are receiving information all the time, and you need to be able to take in this information and respond as necessary. Much of the information that you need to understand comes from regulatory road signs and markings that tell you things that you must do.

The questions in this section are designed to check that you know:

○ The meaning of all the road signs and markings that you might meet when you are driving:

  • Regulatory signs and markings that tell you things you must do;

  • Signs that give you advance warning of when you should take special care; and

  • Motorway signs;

○ The regulations relating to speed;

○ The regulations relating to parking; and

○. The meaning of the various hand signals that a garda might make, and the hand signals you might need to make yourself.

Regulatory traffic signs

Regulatory traffic signs are those that you must obey. Most of them are circular in shape, have a red border and symbols or text in black. The STOP and YIELD signs have unique shapes so that they cannot be confused with any other signs.

What does this sign mean?

Stop your vehicle.

This sign appears at junctions where a minor road joins a major road. You must stop your vehicle completely at a STOP sign.

What must a driver do when this sign is accompanied by a white stop line on the road?

Stop at the line.

What must a driver do when this sign is NOT accompanied by a white stop line on the road?

Stop at the sign.

When accompanied by a STOP sign, the white stop line indicates the point at which you must stop your vehicle. Where a STOP sign is not accompanied by a white stop line, you must stop at the sign.

What does this sign mean at a junction?

Yield to traffic on the major road.

At a junction, the YIELD sign tells you that you must give way to traffic on a major road ahead. This means that you must slow down and be prepared to stop.

What does this sign mean at a roundabout?

Yield to traffic coming from the right.

At a roundabout, the YIELD sign tells you that you must slow down and be prepared to stop. You must yield (give way) to traffic already on the roundabout.

What does this sign mean?

Straight ahead only.

This sign tells you that you must proceed straight ahead. It is usually displayed on the entry to a one-way street.

What does this sign mean?

Turn left only.

This sign tells you that you must turn left. It is usually displayed at a junction where all traffic must turn left – for example, in a one-way system that incorporates a junction.

What does this sign mean?

Turn right only.

This sign tells you that you must turn right. It is usually displayed at a junction where all traffic must turn right – for example, in a one-way system that incorporates a junction.

What does this sign mean?

Turn left ahead.

This sign tells you that you must turn left ahead. It is usually displayed on the approach to a one-way system.

What does this sign mean?

Turn right ahead.

This sign tells you that you must turn right ahead. It is usually displayed on the approach to a one-way system.

What does this sign mean?

Keep left.

This sign tells you that you must keep left. It is usually displayed at a traffic island in the centre of the road.

What does this sign mean?

Keep right.

This sign tells you that you must keep right. It is usually found in a one-way system where the traffic is required to keep to the right.

What does this sign mean?

Pass either side.

This sign tells you that traffic must pass on either side of the traffic island.

What does this sign mean?

No entry.

This sign tells you that you must not proceed in the direction of the arrow. This is displayed to prevent traffic going in the wrong direction – for example, the wrong way up a one-way street.

What does this sign mean?

No right turn.

This sign is displayed at a junction where you may not turn right.

What does this sign mean?

No left turn.

This sign is displayed at a junction where you may not turn left.

What does this sign mean?

U-turn not permitted.

This sign tells you that you are not permitted to make a U-turn. It is displayed at junctions on dual carriageways. U-turns are also not permitted anywhere there is a continuous white line along the centre of the road or on a one-way street.

What does this sign mean?

Maximum speed is 30km/h.

This sign tells you that the maximum legal speed limit permitted for this section of road is 30km/h.

What does this sign mean?

Maximum speed is 50km/h.

This sign tells you that the maximum legal speed limit permitted for this section of road is 50km/h.

What does this sign mean?

Maximum speed is 60km/h.

This sign tells you that the maximum legal speed limit permitted for this section of road is 60km/h.

What does this sign mean?

Maximum speed is 80km/h.

This sign tells you that the maximum legal speed limit permitted for this section of road is 80km/h.

What does this sign mean?

Maximum speed is 100km/h.

This sign tells you that the maximum legal speed limit permitted for this section of road is 100km/h.

What does this sign mean?

Maximum speed is 120km/h.

This sign tells you that the maximum legal speed limit permitted for this section of road is 120km/h.

What do these signs together mean?

Parking permitted at times shown.

These signs tells you that parking is permitted in both directions, but only at the times shown on the information plate.

What does this sign mean?

Parking prohibited.

This sign tells you that parking is prohibited in both directions.

What do these signs together mean?

Clearway – no stopping or parking during the times shown.

A Clearway sign means that no stopping or parking is allowed in this area during the times shown on the information plate.

What does this sign mean?

Disc parking operates during the time shown.

This sign tells you your vehicle must display a parking disc when you park during the hours shown on the information plate.

What does this sign mean?

Appointed rank for taxis.

A Taxi Rank sign indicates that this is an area reserved for taxis, and parking is not permitted there.

What do these signs together mean?

Start of cycle track.

This sign indicates the start of a cycle track. If the cycle track is bounded by a broken white line, other road users should avoid using it wherever possible. If it is bounded by a continuous white line, drivers of cars and other vehicles must not drive on this track.

What does this sign mean?

Shared cycle/pedestrian track.

This sign indicates the start of a track for cyclists and pedestrians only. If the track is bounded by a broken white line, other road users should avoid using it wherever possible. If it is bounded by a continuous white line, drivers of cars and other vehicles must not drive on this track.

What does this sign mean?

Stop for school warden.

This sign is used by a school warden. When the warden raises this sign, you must stop and wait until the schoolchildren have crossed the road.

What do these signs together mean?

Pedestrianised street ahead – traffic not allowed except during times shown.

This sign tells you that there is a pedestrian area ahead and that traffic is not allowed except during the times stated on the information plate.

What does this sign mean?

Maximum permitted weight is 3 tonnes.

This sign tells you that that you must not enter this area if your vehicle is over the stated weight limit.

What does this sign mean?

Vehicle weight restriction is 10 tonnes.

This sign tells you that you must not enter this area if your vehicle is over the stated weight limit. This may be found at a weak bridge. There are no exemptions.

What does this sign mean?

No entry to goods vehicles with five axles or more.

This sign tells you that heavy goods vehicles with five or more axles are not permitted to enter this road.

What does this sign mean?

Maximum permitted height of vehicle is the figure indicated.

This sign tells you that you must not enter this area if your vehicle exceeds the indicated height.

What does this sign mean?

Parking of vehicles exceeding the weight shown is not allowed.

This sign tells you that you must not park in this area if your vehicle is over the weight limit indicated.

What does this sign mean?

No overtaking.

This sign tells you that overtaking is prohibited in this area because it is dangerous to do so.

What do these signs together mean?

Only buses, cyclists and taxis are allowed to use the lane during the hours indicated.

This sign tells you there is a with-flow bus lane ahead – that is, one where the buses move in the same direction as the traffic to their right.

The information plate tells the times when the bus lane is in operation. Only buses, taxis and cyclists may use the bus lane during those hours.

What does this sign mean?

'With flow' bus and cycle lane ahead on left.

This sign tells you there is a with-flow bus lane ahead to the left. Only buses, taxis and cyclists may use the bus lane during the stated operational hours.

What does this sign mean?

'With flow' bus and cycle lane on left.

This sign indicates a with-flow bus lane ahead. Only buses, taxis and cyclists may use the bus lane during the stated operational hours.

What does this sign mean?

Bus and cycle lane ahead on right.

This sign tells you there is a with-flow bus lane ahead to the right. Only buses, taxis and cyclists may use the bus lane during the stated operational hours.

What does this sign mean?

'With flow' bus lane on the right.

This sign indicates a with-flow bus lane ahead to the right. Only buses, taxis and cyclists may use the bus lane during the stated operational hours.

What does this sign mean?

'Contra flow' bus lane ahead.

This sign tells you that you must drive on the left and not use the contra-flow bus lane ahead day or night. A contra-flow bus lane is one where the buses are going in the opposite direction to the traffic on their right.

What does this sign mean?

Tram lane on left.

This sign tells you there e is a tram lane on the left. Be aware that there might be pedestrians in the area and crossing the road.

Tram lane on right.

This sign tells you there is a tram lane ahead to the right. Be aware that there might be pedestrians in the area and crossing the road.

Warning signs

Warning signs give you advance notice of changes in the road layout, of junctions and bends ahead, and of anything that might cause a hazard. Most warning signs are diamond shaped with black symbols on a yellow background.

You don't have to do anything when you see a warning sign, but in many cases you will need to make some change in your driving. For example, you might need to slow down as you approach a sharp bend or when you know there is a school ahead.

What does this sign mean?

Junction ahead with roads of lesser importance.

This sign gives advance warning of a junction ahead with minor roads on either side. Be aware that vehicles may be emerging from the minor roads .

What does this sign mean?

Main road bears to the left.

This sign gives advance warning of a junction with a minor road ahead. The wider arm of the Y indicates the course of the main road.

What does this sign mean?

Staggered crossroads ahead with roads of equal importance.

This sign gives advance warning of a staggered junction ahead with roads to the left and right. Be aware that vehicles may be emerging from these roads.

What does this sign mean?

Crossroads ahead with roads of equal importance.

This sign gives advance warning of a junction with roads of equal importance ahead. At this type of junction you should yield to traffic approaching from the right and traffic already turning.

What does this sign mean?

T-junction ahead with road of equal importance.

This sign gives advance warning of a T-junction ahead with a road of equal importance. You must give way to traffic already on the road you are joining.

What does this sign mean?

Y-junction ahead with roads of equal importance.

This sign gives advance warning of a Y-junction ahead with roads of equal importance. Approach such a junction with caution and be prepared to react to any changes in the traffic situation.

What does this sign mean?

Major road ahead.

This sign gives advance warning of a crossroads junction with a major road ahead. Be prepared to stop.

What does this sign mean?

T-junction ahead with a road of major importance.

This sign gives advance warning of a T-junction with a major road ahead. Be prepared to stop.

What does this sign mean?

Crossroads with dual carriageway ahead.

This sign gives advance warning of a crossroads junction with a dual carriageway ahead. Be prepared to stop and give way to other traffic.

What does this sign mean?

T-junction with dual carriageway ahead.

This sign gives advance warning of a T-junction with a dual carriageway ahead. Be prepared to stop and give way to other traffic.

What does this sign mean?

Traffic merging from the left.

This sign gives advance warning of traffic merging from the left ahead. You should expect vehicles to join from the left ahead and you may need to slow down to allow them to merge.

What does this sign mean?

Traffic merging/diverging ahead.

This sign gives advance warning of roads merging and diverging at the left ahead. You should be prepared for traffic changing direction ahead as vehicles may be entering or exiting at the junctions on the left.

What does this sign mean?

Roundabout ahead.

This sign gives advance warning of a roundabout ahead. You must prepare to yield to vehicles already on the roundabout coming from the right.

What does this sign mean?

Mini-roundabout ahead.

This sign gives advance warning of a mini-roundabout ahead. You must prepare to yield to vehicles already on the roundabout coming from the right.

What does this sign mean?

Dangerous corner ahead.

This sign gives advance warning of a dangerous corner to the left. You should slow down and be prepared to react to any changes in the traffic situation.

What does this sign mean?

Dangerous bend ahead.

This sign gives advance warning of a dangerous bend ahead. You should slow down and be prepared to react to any changes in the traffic situation.

What does this sign mean?

Series of dangerous corners ahead.

This sign gives advance warning of a series of dangerous corners ahead. You should slow down and be prepared to react to any changes in the traffic situation.

What does this sign mean?

Series of dangerous bends ahead.

This sign gives advance warning of a series of dangerous bends ahead. You should slow down and be prepared to react to any changes in the traffic situation.

What does this sign mean?

Sharp change of direction to the right.

This sign gives advance warning of a sharp change of direction to the right. You should slow down as you approach the hazard.

What does this sign mean?

Road narrows on the left.

This sign gives advance warning that the road narrows on the left ahead. You should show caution and prepare to move to the right.

What does this sign mean?

Road narrows on both sides.

This sign gives advance warning that the road is narrowing ahead. You should show caution and prepare to slow down.

What does this sign mean?

Road divides ahead.

This sign gives advance warning that the road divides ahead. You should prepare to move to the left.

What does this sign mean?

Dual carriageway ends.

This sign gives advance warning of the end of a dual carriageway. You will soon be entering a 2-way road.

What does this sign mean?

Two-way traffic ahead.

This sign gives advance warning of two-way traffic ahead, with oncoming traffic in the opposite lane.

What does this sign mean?

Sharp descent ahead.

This sign gives advance warning of a steep downward slope ahead. You should react accordingly by adjusting speed and selecting the appropriate gear.

What does this sign mean?

Sharp ascent ahead.

This sign gives advance warning of a steep upward hill ahead . You should react by selecting the appropriate gear.

What does this sign mean?

Restricted headroom up ahead.

This sign gives advance warning that you are approaching an area of restricted headroom, such as a low bridge.

What does this sign mean?

Overhead electric cables.

This sign gives advance warning of electric cables overhead. Drivers with a high load should be particularly careful.

What does this sign mean?

Level crossing ahead unguarded by gates or barriers.

This sign gives advanced warning of an unguarded level crossing ahead. This is a crossing without gates or barriers and you should cross it with extreme caution.

What does this sign mean?

Level crossing ahead guarded by gates or barriers.

This sign gives advance warning of a railway crossing ahead that is protected by gates or lifting barriers. You should be prepared to stop and follow the required procedure.

What does this sign mean?

Level crossing ahead with lights and barriers.

This sign gives advance warning of a railway crossing ahead that is protected by gates or lifting barriers. You should be prepared to stop and follow the required procedure.

What does this sign mean?

The driver must stop when red lights show.

STOP
nuair a lasann na soilse dearga

**STOP
When
Red Lights
Show**

This sign gives advance warning that you must stop when red lights show. This sign may be displayed at a railway level crossing.

What does this sign mean?

Automatic level crossing ahead.

GO MALL
Crosaire Comhréidh Uathoibrioch

**SLOW
Automatic
Level Crossing**

This sign gives advance warning of automatic level crossing ahead. Prepare to stop.

What does this sign mean?

Sharp rise in the road ahead – for example, a humpback bridge.

This sign gives advance warning of a hump in the road. You should adjust your speed accordingly.

What does this sign mean?

Sharp depression or dip ahead.

This sign gives advance warning of a dip or depression in the road ahead. You should reduce your speed accordingly.

What does this sign mean?

Series of bumps or hollows ahead.

This sign gives advance warning of a series of bumps or hollows ahead. You should reduce your speed accordingly.

What does this sign mean?

Slippery stretch of road ahead.

This sign gives advance warning that there might be a danger of skidding because of an uncertain road surface ahead.

What does this sign mean?

Unprotected quay, canal or river ahead.

This sign gives advance warning of an open water area ahead. You should show caution in this situation.

What does this sign mean?

Traffic signals ahead.

This sign gives advance warning of a traffic light controlled junction ahead where drivers might not see the lights in good time – for example, following a bend in the road.

What does this sign mean?

Accompanied horses and ponies ahead.

This sign gives advance warning that there may be horses on the road ahead. You should show due regard for horses and their riders.

What does this sign mean?

Possibility of cattle or farm animals ahead.

This sign gives advance warning that there may be cattle or other farm animals on the road ahead.

What does this sign mean?

Possibility of sheep ahead.

This sign gives advance warning that there may be sheep on the road ahead.

What does this sign mean?

Possibility of deer or wild animals ahead.

This sign gives advance warning that there may be deer or other wild animals coming onto the roadway.

What does this sign mean?

Pedestrian crossing ahead.

This sign gives advance warning of a pedestrian crossing ahead. You should show caution and be prepared to stop.

What does this sign mean?

School ahead.

This sign gives advance warning of a school ahead. You should adjust your speed accordingly as there may be children in the area.

What does this sign mean?

School children crossing ahead.

This sign gives advance warning that there may be school children crossing the road ahead, and you should be prepared to stop.

What do these signs together mean?

Beware of children crossing.

These signs are usually displayed in residential areas, and they give advance warning that children might be crossing ahead. You should drive with extra caution.

What does this sign mean?

Crosswinds.

This sign gives advance warning that there may be crosswinds ahead. Crosswinds can affect the stability of your vehicle on the road.

What does this sign mean?

Tunnel ahead.

This sign gives advance warning of a tunnel ahead. You should be aware of the procedures to follow when entering a tunnel – such as turning on headlights.

What does this sign mean?

Danger of falling rocks ahead.

This sign gives advance warning that there is a danger of rocks and other debris falling onto the road.

What does this sign mean?

Possibility of low flying aircraft.

This sign gives advance warning that there may be low-flying aircraft in the area. Low-flying aircraft can make a loud noise.

What does this sign mean?

A driver must drive on the left-hand side.

This sign is generally in areas where tourists might be travelling and reminds motorists to drive on the left.

What does this sign mean?

Tramway crossing ahead.

This sign gives advance warning of a tram crossing ahead. You should be prepared to stop and yield to the tram, if required.

What does this sign mean?

Tramway crossing ahead.

This sign gives pedestrians advance warning of a tram crossing where they should look both ways before crossing the road.

What does this sign mean?

Tram track, cyclists beware.

This is an advance warning sign for cyclists to be aware that they are approaching a tram track and that the surface may be slippery.

Motorway signs

Driving on a motorway presents a different set of challenges. In general, traffic is moving faster than on national or regional roads, and you need to plan your journey more carefully in advance.

Only drivers with a full licence may drive on a motorway.

What kind of vehicles are not prohibited by this sign?

Motor homes.

Motor homes are not on the list of vehicles which are prohibited by law from entering a motorway.

What does this sign mean?

Entry to motorway.

This is a motorway information sign telling you that you are entering a motorway.

What does this sign mean?

Motorway ends 500 metres ahead.

This is a motorway information sign that tells you that the motorway will end in 500 metres.

What does this sign mean?

Three hundred meters to the next exit.

What does this sign mean?

200 metres to the next exit.

What does this sign mean?

100 metres to the next exit.

These motorway information signs tell you that the next exit off the motorway is 300, 200 and 100 metres ahead respectively.

What does this sign mean?

End of motorway.

This sign indicates the end of the motorway. You are now leaving the motorway and its restrictions no longer apply.

What does this sign mean when displayed on the approach to a motorway?

Cashier in this lane.

This sign is used at motorway toll plazas to direct traffic into a lane where the toll charge may be paid directly to a cashier. This lane would normally be used by motorists who have neither the exact change nor an electronic tag on their vehicle.

What does this sign mean when displayed on the approach to a motorway?

Coin basket in this lane.

This sign is used at motorway toll plazas to direct traffic into a lane where the toll charge may be paid by putting the exact change into a coin basket. This lane usually has a height barrier fitted to prevent large vehicles using it. This lane is generally a quicker way through the toll plaza than the cashier lane. No change is given at such lanes.

What does this sign mean when displayed on the approach to a motorway?

Electronic toll in this lane.

This sign is used at motorway toll plazas to direct traffic into a lane where the toll charge is collected electronically. When the vehicle passes through the plaza it is identified by means of an electronic tag fitted to the front windscreen. Payment will be collected via the user's account. Only vehicles fitted with the tags are allowed to use those lanes.

Road works signs

Road works present a variety of hazards that you need to take into account when you are driving. Always drive with extra care through road works, and take note of the particular signs that are posted.

Like other warning signs, most road works signs are diamond shaped and have a black border and black symbols or text on an orange background.

What does this sign mean?

Roadworks ahead.

This warning sign tells you that there are roadworks ahead. You should approach with caution and be alert for a change in road surface, and for the presence of machinery and road workers.

What does this sign mean?

Uneven surface ahead.

This roadworks warning sign tells you that the surface ahead is uneven and you should approach with caution.

What does this sign mean?

Slippery road.

This roadworks warning sign tells you that the surface ahead is slippery and that there is an increased risk of skidding .

What does this sign mean?

Road narrows from left.

This roadworks warning sign tells you that the road narrows suddenly from the left creating a potential hazard.

What does this sign mean?

Road narrows from right.

This roadworks warning sign tells you that the road narrows suddenly from the right creating a potential hazard.

What does this sign mean?

Road narrows on both sides.

This roadworks warning sign tells you that the road narrows on both sides creating a potential hazard. Drive with extra care.

What does this sign mean?

Flagman ahead.

This roadworks warning sign tells you that the traffic sequence ahead is controlled manually or by an automatic system.

What does this sign mean?

Temporary traffic signals ahead.

This roadworks warning sign tells you that temporary traffic signals are in use ahead. You should approach with caution and comply with the signal displayed.

What does this sign mean?

Two-way traffic.

This roadworks warning sign tells you that there is two-way traffic in operation.

What does this sign mean?

Nearside lane of two closed.

This roadworks warning sign tells you that that the lane on the left ahead is closed. If you are in the left lane you will need to move to the right when it is safe to do so.

What does this sign mean?

Nearside lane of three closed.

This roadworks warning sign tells you the left-hand lane of three is closed ahead. If you are in the left lane you will need to move to the right when it is safe to do so.

What does this sign mean?

Loose chippings on road.

This roadworks warning sign tells you that the road ahead has been resurfaced and there may be loose chippings. You should reduce speed while driving through this area as the loose chippings could affect your vehicle's road holding and braking .

What does this sign mean?

Offside lane closed ahead.

This roadworks warning sign tells you that the extreme right-hand lane is closed ahead. If you are in this lane, you need to move to the left when it is safe to do so. The offside lane is the lane closest to the centre of the road.

What does this sign mean?

Traffic queues likely ahead.

This roadworks warning sign tells you that there may be traffic queues ahead, possibly due to temporary traffic lights at the works. Proceed with caution.

What does this sign mean?

Uneven surface .

This roadworks warning sign tells you that the road surface may be uneven, possibly due to the resurfacing of part of a lane. Proceed with caution.

What does this sign mean?

Obstruction between lanes ahead.

This roadworks warning sign tells you that there is an obstruction in the centre of the road ahead and that two-way traffic will separate to avoid it.

What does this sign mean?

Pedestrians cross to the right.

This roadworks warning sign tells pedestrians to cross to the right as the footpath may be closed at this point.

At roadworks, what does this sign mean?

Proceed with caution.

This is the sign telling you to proceed with caution through road works. It may be displayed by a flagman or by an automated system.

At roadworks, what does this sign mean?

Stop before or at the sign.

This is a roadworks warning sign telling you to stop. It may be displayed by a flagman or by an automated system.

What do these signs together mean?

End of detour.

These roadworks warning signs indicate that a detour has ended and that you are back on the original route.

What does this sign mean?

Traffic must cross over to the left-hand lane.

This roadworks warning sign tells you that the course of the road will return to the left ahead. This usually appears after a stretch where traffic was diverted to a right-hand lane.

What does this sign mean?

Traffic must cross over to the right-hand lane.

This roadworks warning sign tells you that the course of the road will temporarily cross the central reserve to the right.

What does this sign mean?

Start of central reserve or obstruction.

This roadworks warning sign tells you that two-way traffic will separate to avoid an obstruction.

What does this sign mean?

End of central reserve or obstruction.

This roadworks warning sign tells you that traffic that was separated will revert to two-way road.

Hand signals

You need to be able to interpret correctly the hand signals that other road users make, and there are times when you might need to give clear hand signals.

You also need to know the meaning of hand signals given by a garda.

What does this hand signal mean?

The cyclist intends to move out or turn right.

This hand signal tells other road users that the cyclist intends to either move out or make a right turn.

What does this hand signal mean?

The cyclist intends to slow down or stop.

This hand signal informs other road users that cyclist intends to slow down or stop. This may indicate that the cyclist is aware of some hazard ahead, so drive with extra care.

What does this hand signal mean?

The cyclist intends to go straight on.

This hand signal informs other road users that the cyclist intends to proceed straight ahead at a junction and drivers should show caution.

What does this hand signal mean?

The cyclist intends to turn left.

This hand signal informs other road users that the cyclist intends to make a left-hand turn.

What does this hand signal mean?

The cyclist intends to turn right.

This hand signal informs other road users that the cyclist intends to turn right.

What does this hand signal mean?

The cyclist intends to turn left.

This hand signal informs other road users that the cyclist intends to turn left.

What does this hand signal mean?

The driver intends to turn left.

This hand signal informs other road users that the driver intends to turn left and the vehicle will change direction.

What does this hand signal mean?

The driver intends to move out or turn right.

This hand signal informs other road users that the driver intends to move out or turn right and the vehicle will change direction.

What does this hand signal mean?

The driver intends to slow down or stop.

This hand signal informs other road users that the driver intends to slow down or stop and following traffic should be prepared to slow down also.

What does this hand signal mean?

The driver intends to turn left.

This hand signal informs other road users or a garda directing traffic (facing this vehicle), that the driver intends to make a left hand turn.

What does this hand signal mean?

The driver intends to turn right.

This hand signal informs other road users or a garda directing traffic (facing this vehicle) that the driver intends to turn right.

What does this hand signal mean?

The driver intends to move straight ahead.

This hand signal informs other road users or a garda directing traffic that the driver intends to proceed straight ahead.

What does this Garda signal mean?

Stop if approaching from the front.

When approaching a garda giving this signal you must stop.

What does this Garda signal mean?

Stop if approaching from behind.

When approaching a garda giving this signal you must stop.

What does this Garda signal mean?

Stop if approaching from either the front or behind.

When approaching a garda giving this signal you must stop.

What does this Garda signal mean?

The Garda is beckoning on traffic approaching from either side.

When approaching a garda giving this signal you may proceed.

What does this Garda signal mean?

Traffic approaching from the front may proceed.

When approaching a garda giving this signal you may proceed.

Road markings

In addition to knowing what all the regulatory road signs mean, you also have to understand the meaning of road markings and act accordingly.

What does this road marking indicate?

Zebra crossing.

A zebra crossing is a designated area for pedestrians to cross the road. As a driver you must always yield to pedestrians on a zebra crossing.

What does this road marking mean?

A driver must not enter unless turning right or the exit is clear.

You must not enter the yellow box junction unless you can clear it without stopping or unless you are turning right and are prevented from doing so by oncoming traffic.

What does this road marking mean?

No parking in this area.

White zig zag lines indicate that you are approaching a pedestrian crossing. You must not park or overtake within this area.

What does this road marking and information plate together mean?

Parking not allowed at the times shown.

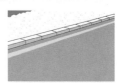

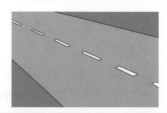

A single yellow line along the edge of a road means that you must not park there during the times shown on the accompanying information plate.

What does this road marking mean?

A driver must not cross the broken white line unless it is safe to do so.

A broken white line along the centre of the road means you must not cross the line unless it is safe to do so when overtaking or passing.

What do white arrows painted on the road indicate?

The lane drivers should use for the direction
they intend to take.

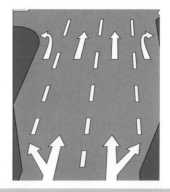

When approaching a junction you must select the appropriate lane for the direction you want to
go. The appropriate lane may be marked by directional arrows. Make sure you change lane only
when it is safe to do so.

What does this road marking mean?

A driver must not cross the line.

Vehicles may not cross or straddle the line.

No U-turn allowed.

No overtaking.

No parking allowed.

A continuous white line is marked on the road where it is dangerous to carry out any of the
above manoeuvres. This is because it may be in a built-up area or an area of restricted vision,
such as on a bend or on a section of road which has dangerous junctions joining it.

What could this road marking mean?

Continuous white lines ahead.

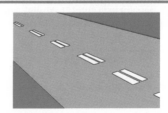

Double broken white lines along the centre of the road alert you to continuous white lines
ahead. Do not cross them unless it is safe to do so.

If driving from A to B, what do these road markings mean?

A driver may overtake if it is safe to do so.

Where there is a broken white line and a continuous white line along the centre of the road, you must obey the line that is nearest to you. In this case you may cross the lines as long as it is safe to do so.

If driving from A to B, what do these road markings mean?

A driver may not cross the lines to overtake.

Where there is a broken white line and a continuous white line along the centre of the road, you must obey the line that is nearest to you. In this case you may not cross the lines .

What does this road marking mean?

No entry.

This road marking indicates the 'wrong' end of a one-way street. You may not enter this street.

What does this road marking mean?

Parking prohibited at all times.

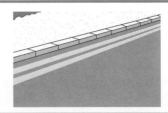

A double yellow line along the edge of the road means parking is not allowed at any time.

What does the broken yellow line road marking mean?

The edge of the carriageway or hard shoulder.

A single broken yellow line along the side of the road marks the edge of the carriageway/hard shoulder. This is normally for the use of pedestrians and cyclists. As a driver, however, you may use it briefly to allow faster traffic to overtake, but only where it is safe to do so.

Traffic lights

You need to know the meaning of all traffic light signals, including those with filter arrows.

What does this traffic light mean?

Stop, unless it is unsafe to do so.

When the traffic light is showing amber you must not go beyond the stop line unless you are so close to the traffic lights that stopping would be dangerous.

What does this traffic light mean?

The driver may proceed in the direction of the green arrow if the way is clear.

A green arrow (filter light) means that traffic may proceed in the direction of the arrow if it is safe to do so.

What does this traffic light mean?

Left turning traffic may proceed if the way is clear.

A green arrow (filter light) means that traffic may proceed in the direction of the arrow if it is safe to do so.

What does this traffic light mean?

Traffic must stop at the traffic light.

A red light means STOP. You must not go beyond the stop line or (if there is no stop line) beyond the light.

What does this traffic light mean?

Traffic may proceed if the way is clear.

You may proceed on a green traffic light if it is safe to do so.

What colour traffic light comes on after the green?

Amber only.

The normal sequence of traffic lights is red–green–amber.

What does a flashing left amber arrow at a traffic light mean?

A driver may turn left but yield to traffic
on the other road.

A flashing left amber arrow at a junction means you may proceed left but must give way to
pedestrians and traffic already coming through the junction on the other road.

When traffic lights are green, when should a driver not proceed?

When by doing so the vehicle would block the junction.

Although a green traffic light means proceed with caution, you should not enter a junction if the
way is not clear or if by doing so you would cause an obstruction to other road users.

What colour traffic light comes on after a non-flashing amber light?

Red only.

The normal sequence of traffic lights is red–green–amber.

What do flashing amber lights at a pelican crossing mean?

Stop and give way to pedestrians – proceed if the way is clear.

A flashing amber light at a pelican crossing means you must yield to pedestrians. You may
proceed, however, if the crossing is clear.

Speed limits

You must know the speed limits that apply to different types of road and to different types of vehicle. Always drive at a speed that is safe and appropriate to the road you are on. Never exceed the posted speed limits.

What is the maximum permissible speed for cars or motorcycles on motorways?

120km/h.

It is illegal to exceed 120km/h when driving on a motorway.

What is the maximum permissible speed for cars or motorcycles on single carriageway national roads?

100km/h.

It is illegal to exceed 100km/h when driving on a single carriageway national road.

What is the maximum permissible speed of a car towing a caravan (or trailer) on national primary roads?

80km/h.

What is the maximum permissible speed of a car towing a caravan (or trailer) on a motorway?

80km/h.

When towing a caravan or trailer, it is illegal to exceed 80km/h – excessive speed will make such a vehicle unstable.

Regulations relating to parking

Before you park a vehicle, you need to make sure that it is safe and legal to do so in the place you have chosen. A vehicle parked in an inappropriate place may be a serious hazard to other road users. Make sure you know all of the regulations relating to parking.

Where must a driver not park?

Where there is a continuous white line along the centre of the road.

It is an offence to park at the side of a road that has a single or double continuous white line along its centre. Parking on such a road could create an obstruction and may cause inconvenience or danger to other road users.

For what distance before a zebra crossing is parking prohibited?

15 metres.

It is an offence to park 15 metres before or 5 metres beyond a pedestrian crossing. Parking in this manner may restrict the zone of vision of drivers approaching the crossing and endanger pedestrians.

Within what distance of a junction is parking prohibited?

5 metres.

It is an offence to park within 5 metres of a road junction unless parking spaces are clearly marked. Parking in that area may restrict the zone of vision of drivers approaching the junction and may cause an obstruction to large vehicles wishing to turn.

When may a driver park a vehicle in a loading bay?

When the driver is the driver of a goods vehicle and is loading or unloading.

Loading bays are provided to enable goods vehicles to load or unload goods, up to a maximum of 30 minutes. Only goods vehicles are permitted to use loading bays.

Is a driver permitted to park at an entrance to a property?

Yes, with the property owner's consent.

You may park across the entrance to a property only with the owner's consent. Parking across an entrance may cause inconvenience and danger to persons entering or leaving the property.

When is parking permitted on a footpath?

It is never permitted to park on a footpath.

It is always an offence to park on a footpath. Where a vehicle is parked on a footpath, pedestrians may have to step onto the road to go around the vehicle and so place themselves in danger.

When is double parking permitted?

Double parking is never permitted.

Double parking is never permitted. Parking is never permitted where it might interfere in any way with the normal flow of traffic or obstruct or endanger other road users.

When is parking permitted at a taxi rank?

Parking at a taxi rank is prohibited.

Stopping or parking within an area marked as a taxi rank is prohibited as this may obstruct taxis entering or leaving the rank.

When is parking permitted at a sharp bend?

Parking is never permitted at a sharp bend.

Parking is never permitted where it might interfere in any way with the normal flow of traffic or obstruct or endanger other road users – for example, by forcing other drivers into the path of oncoming traffic.

When is parking permitted on the brow of a hill?

Parking on the brow of a hill is never allowed.

Parking on the brow of a hill or on a humpbacked bridge is prohibited. Parking in such a place may restrict the zone of vision of drivers approaching the hill and force them into the path of oncoming traffic.

Regulations relating to pedestrians

Pedestrians are the most vulnerable road users, and as a driver you need to be extra careful where there are pedestrians.

If there is no footpath, where must a pedestrian walk?

Right-hand side of the road.

Where there is no footpath provided, pedestrians should walk on the right-hand side of the road facing oncoming traffic. Drivers should be aware of the *Rules of the Road* for pedestrians, drive with caution and be prepared to react to any changes in the traffic situation.

On a narrow busy road, what rules apply to pedestrians when walking?

Walk in single file.

Pedestrians should walk in single file on busy narrow roads. Drivers should be aware of the *Rules of the Road* for pedestrians, drive with caution and be prepared to react to any changes in the traffic situation.

When should pedestrians wear reflective clothing at night?

At all times outside well-lit urban areas.

Outside built-up areas, pedestrians should wear reflective clothing at all times when walking at night. This is particularly important where there is no street lighting and no footpath for pedestrians.

What road users must comply with traffic lights (including pedestrian lights)?

All road users.

As road users, pedestrians must comply with traffic controls.

Drivers should be aware that traffic lights and pedestrian lights can be combined at junctions and should show caution and consideration to pedestrians.

Other regulatory matters

There are a number of other regulatory matters that you need to know about. Mostly these are regulations that guide our behaviour and help ensure the safety of all road users.

What does this marker board on a large vehicle indicate?

Overhanging load.

This marker board is displayed on heavy goods vehicle loads to alert other road users when the load or equipment overhangs the front or rear of the vehicle by more than 2 metres.

When are lighting up hours?

From just after dusk to just before dawn.

Lighting up hours are defined as the period of time during which drivers should turn on dipped headlights in order to be seen. This period normally starts half an hour after sunset and ends half an hour before sunrise.

What lights should a vehicle show at dusk?

Dipped headlights.

Drivers need to see and be seen during all periods of low light levels – for example, at dusk and dawn and in some bad weather conditions. At times of low light, you should turn on dipped headlights.

The Road Safety Authority recommends that motorcyclists and drivers turn on their dipped headlights or daytime running lights during daylight hours.

What do rumble strips warn a driver of?

A danger immediately ahead or to the side.

Rumble strips are a patterning in the surface of the roadway that causes a rumbling sound when you drive over them. The purpose of them is to warn you to of a potential danger ahead or to the side.

What is the purpose of traffic calming measures?

To slow down traffic in the vicinity.

The purpose of traffic calming measures is to slow down fast-moving traffic to a speed more suitable for the area they are entering. These measures are usually found in rural areas on the entry points to towns or villages.

When may a trailer be towed on a public road without a rear number plate?

Never, a number plate must always be displayed.

The law requires all motorised vehicles to display a rear number plate that is clean and legible.

When may you pass another vehicle on the left-hand side?

When the vehicle in front is signalling to turn right or in slow moving lanes of traffic.

Normally you must overtake on the right. There are, however, circumstances where you may overtake on the left – for example, when the vehicle has moved out and signalled to turn right.

Who can use a signed cycle track accompanied by a continuous white line on the left-hand side?

What traffic may drive along on a cycle lane accompanied by a broken while line?

Cyclists and users of motorised wheelchairs.

A cycle track is for the use of cyclists and motorised wheelchairs only. No other vehicles may cross into or over a mandatory cycle track unless this is necessary in order to leave or enter a side road or a property adjacent to the cycle track.

When must drivers stop at a railway level crossing controlled by lights and barriers?

When the red lights start to flash.

You are legally required to stop at a level crossing when the red lights start to flash and the warning bells sound. You must wait for all barriers to open fully before proceeding.

At a level crossing with unattended gates, what should a driver do?

Open both gates before proceeding to cross.

At a level crossing with unattended gates a driver must stop, look for trains and listen for the sound of a horn or approaching trains. If it is safe, open both gates, complete the crossing and then close both gates.

What lights indicate a zebra crossing?

Flashing amber beacons.

A zebra crossing is indicated by amber flashing beacons on poles and black and white stripes on the road. You must stop for pedestrians on the crossing and for those about to cross.

What do flashing amber arrows indicate?

Drivers should proceed in the direction indicated.

When you meet a flashing amber arrow, you should proceed in the direction indicated provided it is safe to do so. Large flashing amber arrows can be found at roadworks on dual carriageways and motorways.

What do temporary traffic lights at road works mean?

A driver must comply with the lights at all times.

You must comply with any temporary traffic lights used to control vehicle movements at or near road works.

It is an offence not to obey these lights.

For the duration of the roadworks.

Temporary speed limits at road works apply for a limited period of time. When road works are completed, normal speed limits apply.

Alert driving and consideration for other road users

When you are driving, the traffic situation is changing constantly, and different kinds of hazard can arise with or without warning. You need to remain alert at all times and show consideration for all other road users.

The questions in this section test your knowledge in a number of areas:

Illustrated traffic situations	These are typical of the kind of situations that you need to be alert to when driving.
Anticipation of hazards	Anticipation skills help you identify and avoid hazards on the road.
Consideration for other road users	Good drivers always display consideration for other road users.
Alertness to danger	You need to remain alert to potential danger at all times.

Illustrated traffic situations

Every time you go on the road you meet different traffic situations and potential hazards, and you need to maintain your concentration at all times so that you will make the right and safe decisions every time.

What is the correct action to take in this situation?

Keep a close eye on children. If necessary give a warning signal and be prepared to brake in good time.

Because it is difficult to predict children's behaviour, you should always be prepared to react to a change in the traffic situation or to stop.

An approaching driver notices that the boy on the children's bicycle has said goodbye to his friend. What is the correct action for the driver to take?

Be prepared for the boy setting off at any moment without paying attention to the vehicle.

Because it is difficult to predict children's behaviour, you should always be prepared to react to a change in the traffic situation or to stop.

As the driver of the car, which conduct is correct?

A driver may proceed with caution.

You may proceed, but you should be aware of the presence of the motorcyclist. You should always be prepared to react to a change in the traffic situation – for example, the motorcyclist might not have seen your vehicle.

What should the car driver do in this situation?

The driver must allow the cyclist to proceed.

When you are turning right from a major road to a minor road, you must yield to oncoming traffic, and you should proceed only when it is safe to do so.

What must a driver be prepared for in this situation?

One of the children could turn back to collect the ball from the roadway.

Because it is difficult to predict children's behaviour, you should always be prepared to react to a change in the traffic situation and be prepared to stop.

When approaching the pedestrian crossing, what should the driver do in this situation?

Slow down in good time and be prepared to stop.

When there are pedestrians at or near a zebra crossing, you should slow down on approach and be prepared to stop to allow the pedestrians to cross safely.

What should the driver do in this situation?

The driver must yield to the yellow car on
the roundabout.

When you reach the roundabout, you must give way to traffic approaching from the right
– unless signs, road markings or traffic lights tell you otherwise.

What should the car driver do in this situation?

The car driver must allow the motorcycle
to proceed.

When you are turning right from a major road to a minor road, you must yield to oncoming
traffic. You should proceed only when it is safe to do so.

What should the driver do in this situation?

The driver may turn in front of the other
two cars.

When you are turning right from a major road to a minor road, you must yield to oncoming
traffic and only proceed when it is safe to do so. However, the drivers on the minor roads must
give way to the traffic on the major road.

What should a driver be alert to in this area?

Pedestrians may cross between parked cars.

When driving in a built-up area, you should drive with caution and be prepared to react to pedestrians crossing from between parked vehicles.

What should the driver do if there are children playing at the edge of the roadway?

Reduce speed, drive cautiously and remain ready to brake.

Because it is difficult to predict children's behaviour, you should always be prepared to react to a change in the traffic situation and be prepared to stop.

What should the driver do in this situation?

The driver may cross first with caution.

On approaching a crossroads you should check the road sign to see which traffic has priority and be prepared for emerging traffic from either side. Vehicles do not have an automatic right of way on the road. The overriding rule is to proceed with caution in all circumstances.

What should the driver do in this situation?

The driver may proceed first.

You may turn right if there no oncoming traffic but you should also be aware that there might be traffic emerging from the minor roads.

What should the driver do in this situation?

The driver must allow the blue truck to proceed.

When you are turning right from a major road to a minor road, you must yield to oncoming traffic and proceed only when it is safe to do so. You should also be aware that there might be traffic emerging from the minor road.

What should a driver be conscious of in this situation?

People crossing the street at the rear of the bus.

You should always read the road ahead and be prepared to react to the changing traffic situation. In particular, you should be aware that pedestrians might emerge at the rear of the bus.

In this situation you should also look out for pedestrians making their way towards the waiting bus.

The silver car is overtaking the parked red car, what should the driver do in this situation?

Reduce speed considerably and be ready to stop.

You should read the road and be extra careful while driving through an area where children might be playing. When a ball bounces out on the road you should expect that a child might follow to retrieve the ball.

What should a driver be aware of in this situation?

Pedestrians may leave the traffic island without paying attention.

You should read the road ahead and expect extra pedestrian activity when the tram is at the stop.

The driver is following these two vehicles and wishes to overtake. What must the driver consider before overtaking here?

The driver's field of view is not good enough to allow safe overtaking.

You should always make sure that the road ahead is clear so that there is enough distance to allow you to overtake and get back to the correct side of the road without forcing any other road user to alter speed or course. In this case, the brow of the hill is too close to allow a driver to overtake safely.

What should a driver be aware of when approaching a vehicle which is attempting to park?

That the vehicle being parked may move out without warning.

When you approach a vehicle that is being parked on the roadway, you should be aware that its driver will probably be concentrating on parking the vehicle and may not be aware of moving out into the road to correct its position.

What should the driver allow for when following the bus on an icy road?

A longer braking distance.

When driving in icy conditions, you should always reduce speed and allow a bigger gap to the vehicle in front in order to be able to stop safely if necessary.

What should the driver of the silver car do before turning left?

Allow the cyclist heading straight on to pass.

Do not overtake a cyclist as you approach a junction at which you are turning left. The cyclist might be continuing ahead. Cyclists are vulnerable road users and may be unstable in slow-moving traffic and at junctions. Give them more room.

What lights should a driver use in fog?

Front and rear fog lights along with dipped headlights.

When driving in fog you should switch on your front and rear fog lights along with dipped headlights. You should not drive in fog with full beam headlights on.

What should the driver be most conscious of in this situation?

The pedestrian may suddenly cross the road in front of the vehicle.

It is often difficult to predict other road users' behaviour. Where there are parked vehicles on both sides of the road you should approach with caution, and be prepared to react to a change in the traffic situation and to stop.

What should the driver do when approaching this situation?

Reduce speed and remain ready to brake since the girl on foot could suddenly cross the road.

It is often difficult to predict other road users' behaviour. You should anticipate that if the pedestrian steps onto the road, the silver car will stop suddenly.

What should the driver do?

The driver should allow the yellow car
to proceed.

At a cross junction of equal importance the traffic approaching from the right has priority. It is
important to understand that the right of way is not an absolute right. You must proceed with
caution while showing regard for other road users.

Which car, if any, is parked incorrectly?

Both cars.

It is an offence to park within 15 metres before or 5 metres after a pedestrian crossing. Parking
in this manner may restrict the zone of vision of drivers approaching the crossing and endanger
pedestrians.

What should a driver be aware of in this situation?

The cyclist will move onto the roadway
without paying attention to moving traffic.

You should show extra care when approaching cyclists who are about to exit from a cycle lane
and join the roadway.

A driver wants to pull out of a driveway and turn right onto the road. At the same time a cyclist is approaching from the right and a pedestrian wants to cross. Who must wait?

The driver must wait.

By law you must give way to other road users, including pedestrians and cyclists, when you are entering or leaving a driveway.

What action should the driver take?

Stop at the Stop line.

By law you must stop at a Stop line (or at a Stop sign if there is no Stop line), and wait for other traffic to clear before proceeding.

What should a driver do when travelling behind this vehicle?

Reduce speed and prepare to stop if necessary.

You should always read the road ahead and be prepared to react to the changing traffic situation as you approach junctions.

How should a driver overtake the cyclist in this situation?

By crossing the broken white line.

Where there are two lines in the centre of the road, you must obey the one closest to you. So, if the closest line is a broken white line, by law you may overtake, so long as it is safe to do so.

What does a broken white line in the centre of the road mean?

A driver may straddle or cross the broken line in order to avoid an obstruction or to overtake.

By law, you may cross a broken white line to overtake or avoid an obstruction, as long as it is safe to do so.

The driver intends to turn left at this junction – what should the driver do?

Allow the cyclist to continue before turning left.

Do not overtake a cyclist as you approach a junction at which you are turning left. The cyclist might be continuing ahead. Cyclists are vulnerable road users and may be unstable in slow-moving traffic and at junctions. Give them more room.

Why might it be dangerous to drive on a poorly-lit street?

Pedestrians crossing in a dark area might be difficult to see.

It may be difficult to make out poorly lit vehicles in the dark areas.

When you are driving along a poorly-lit street, you should take extra care – vulnerable road users such as pedestrians might not be so easy to see. You should always be prepared to react to any change in the traffic situation and to hazards such as those posed by unlit parked vehicles.

The driver intends to turn right at this junction – what should the driver do?

Stop at the line.

Proceed after the bus and motorcycle have passed.

When you are turning right at a junction, you should yield to traffic on the major road, and to oncoming traffic at the junction.

You must stop at the line where a junction is controlled by a Stop sign and Stop line. Do not proceed until it is safe to do so.

The driver intends to turn right at this junction – what should the driver do?

Allow the cyclist and bus to proceed.

When you are turning right from a side road onto a major road from a side road, you must yield to both oncoming traffic and to traffic on the major road.

There is a strong wind blowing from the left. The driver intends to overtake this truck. When is the driver most exposed to danger?

When the driver enters the slipstream of the truck.

Be aware that the stability of your vehicle could be seriously affected when you are overtaking a large vehicle in windy conditions. The slipstream of the large vehicle is in the area immediately behind it where you are sheltered from the oncoming wind.

What should a driver do when approaching traffic lights that change from green to amber?

Stop, unless it is unsafe to do so.

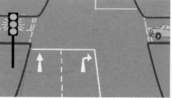

When you are approaching a set of traffic lights showing green, you should take care and be prepared to stop if the amber light comes on.

What should a driver do if dazzled by the lights of an oncoming vehicle?

Look to the left-hand edge of the roadway and if necessary reduce speed.

If you are dazzled by the lights of oncoming traffic, turn your eyes to the left edge of the road. If necessary, stop and allow your eyes to recover before driving on.

When intending to turn right as shown, what should the car driver do?

Wait and allow the oncoming vehicle to pass.

Proceed before the truck.

When you are turning right from a main road onto a side road, you must by law give way to oncoming traffic on a main road.

When you are driving on a main road, you have priority over traffic emerging from side roads. But it is important to understand that the right of way is not an absolute right and you must proceed with caution and showing regard for other road users.

What danger should a driver allow for over the brow of this hill?

There may be a slow moving vehicle in your lane.

A vehicle may be broken down.

An oncoming vehicle may be straddling part of your lane.

There may be oncoming pedestrians.

There may be livestock on the road.

There may be hedge-cutting taking place.

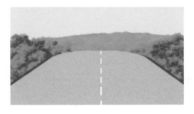

On the approach to the brow of a hill you should be extra careful and be prepared to react to a change in the traffic situation.

What should a driver be aware of in this situation?

There may be a car hidden from view in front of the bus.

On approach to an area with a restricted view you should be extra careful and be prepared to react to a change in the traffic situation.

What should a driver do when continuing straight ahead in the middle lane?

Slow down and allow the driver in front to change lanes.

You should always keep a safe distance from the vehicle in front especially when it is slowing down or stopping.

What should a driver be aware of when following the motorcyclist, and the white car is reversing onto the road?

The motorcyclist may suddenly brake.

The driver following the motorcycle may need a longer braking distance than normal.

You should always keep a safe distance from the vehicle in front if it is slowing down or stopping. Always read the road and be prepared to react correctly to changes in the traffic ahead.

What should a driver do on the approach to this situation?

Reduce speed and stop if necessary.

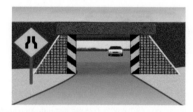

When road priority is unclear you might have to yield to oncoming vehicles. Never drive a vehicle into an area that it might not be able to clear or where it could cause an obstruction or bottleneck.

When driving on a cobblestone road why should you take extra care?

The road surface is uneven and road
grip varies.

When driving on a road with tram lines why should a driver take extra care?

Driving on the tracks can reduce tyre grip.

Different road surfaces can affect your vehicle's grip on the road and its stopping distances. You
should be aware of this when driving on different surfaces – for example over cobblestones or
tram tracks.

After a heavy downpour, why should a driver keep a greater distance from the
vehicle in front?

Because wheel-spray may impair visibility.

Because stopping distances are greater.

Heavy rain can affect how well you can see and how well you can be seen by other road users.
On a wet road surface, your tyres do not grip the road surface as well as in dry conditions and
your stopping distance is increased. For these reasons you should slow down in heavy rain and
keep a greater distance from the vehicle in front.

When driving on this one-way street with vehicles parked on both sides, what
should a driver be prepared for?

A vehicle door may open on either
side of the street.

Pedestrians crossing between the vehicles.

When driving on a one-way street, you should be extra careful and be prepared to react to a
change in the traffic situation.

Why must a driver be particularly careful here?

Because there is an increased danger of
skidding.

Where there are fallen leaves on the road surface, your tyres might have reduced grip on the
road surface and your braking distances might be greater.

What should a driver do in this situation when intending to turn left?

Wait and allow both pedestrians to cross.

By law you must yield to pedestrians already crossing at a junction. Pedestrians are vulnerable
road users and you should be extra careful driving at places where pedestrians are attempting to
cross the road.

What should a driver do when turning right at this junction?

Allow the red car to proceed.

When you are turning right from a main road into a side road, you must give way to oncoming
traffic on the main road even if they are turning left into the same road.

What should the car driver be aware of in this situation?

Oncoming traffic may cut the corner.

Animals could suddenly appear on the road ahead.

When you are approaching a bend or corner with a restricted view you should slow down if necessary and be prepared to react to any changes in the traffic situation.

What should a driver be aware of when driving at night along a shopping street with many different light sources?

Traffic lights may be difficult to distinguish from the other bright lights.

When driving at night in an area where there is a variety of light sources, you need to be extra careful, as potential hazards might be more difficult to see.

What should a driver be most aware of in this situation?

Children may unexpectedly run out from between parked cars.

When driving in a residential area you need to take account of the danger you might pose to children playing. You should always observe warning signs relating to children and drive accordingly.

What should a driver do in this situation?

Reduce speed and be prepared to stop as other children could follow.

You should always be aware of other road users especially children, who can be unpredictable and show no road sense. You should drive with extra care in areas where there are children about – for example, near schools, playgrounds and in residential areas.

In this situation who should wait?

The driver behind the stopped van should wait.

When you are overtaking a parked vehicle or obstruction, you should yield to oncoming vehicles so that they don't have to slow down or take evasive action.

In this situation, who should wait?

The driver in the red car should wait.

A vehicle driving on the main road has priority over vehicles emerging from side roads. However, you must understand that the right of way is not an absolute right of way and you should slow down and be considerate of other road users at all times.

What should a driver be aware of when following the cyclist who is approaching a parked car?

The cyclist may overtake the parked car on the right.

You should always read the road ahead and be prepared to react to changing traffic situations. In this scenario, you should allow the cyclist ahead to overtake the parked car before you do.

In this situation, should a driver overtake the cyclists?

No, the driver cannot see clearly ahead.

You should always read the road ahead and be prepared to react to changing traffic situations.

In this scenario you should wait for a safe opportunity to overtake, and not do so when approaching a bend.

What should a driver be prepared for in this situation?

The cyclist ahead may move out to turn right at the junction.

When approaching cyclists to overtake them, you should be aware that they might change direction or stop.

What should a driver do in this situation?

Allow the pedestrian to cross the road.

When approaching a zebra crossing, you must yield to pedestrians already on or about to cross the road.

What should a driver be aware of in this situation?

A dangerous right-hand bend ahead.

You should always read the road ahead and be prepared to react to changing traffic situations – in this case paying attention to the warning sign clearly indicating a right-hand bend ahead.

What must a driver be prepared for in this situation?

Turning left ahead because of road works.

When you are approaching road works, you should be prepared to divert around or through them and drive at a slower speed. At road works, the road surface may be uneven or dirty.

What should a driver who wants to turn right do in this situation?

Proceed straight ahead or turn left.

As you approach a junction where you want to turn right, you should read the road ahead and take up the correct position for turning in good time.

Which vehicle is in the correct position to make a right turn from the major road into the minor road?

Car 3 is in the correct position to make a right turn.

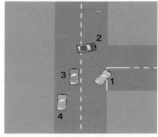

The correct position from which to turn right from a major road to a minor road is just left of centre. You should take up the correct position in good time and avoid cutting the corner or 'swan necking' – that is going beyond the turning point as car (2) is in the picture.

Which vehicle is in the correct position to make a left turn from a minor road onto a major road?

Car 2 is in the correct position to make a left turn.

The correct position from which to turn left from a minor road to a major road is to keep as close to the left-hand side of the roadway as you can safely. When turning left, do not swing wide or mount the kerb.

Which vehicle is in the correct position to take the 3rd exit (the road to the right) at this roundabout?

Car 4 is in the correct position to take the 3rd exit.

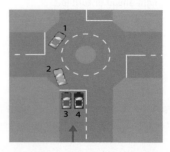

When approaching a roundabout to take an exit to the right (in this case the 3rd exit) you should generally approach in the right-hand lane and keep to the right on the roundabout until it is time to change lanes to exit the roundabout.

Which vehicle is in the correct position to make a right turn from a minor road onto a major road?

Car 1 is in the correct position to turn right.

The correct position from which to turn right from a minor road to a major road is just left of centre of the road. You should take up the correct position in good time and complete the turn by entering the left-hand side of the major road.

Driver behaviour and anticipation

Having good anticipation skills means scanning the road ahead and always being aware of the potential for hazards.

What should the driver do when there is a sharp dip in the road ahead?

Reduce speed, keep to the left and be alert for hazards ahead.

As you approach a sharp dip in the road, you should be aware that there might be hidden dangers ahead. For example, there might be pedestrians, cyclists or other approaching traffic, or the road could be flooded in the dip. You should always read the road ahead and be prepared to react to changing traffic situations – you might need to reduce your speed and drive with extra care.

What should a driver do if they see a red warning triangle on the road?

The driver should slow down and expect a hazard up ahead.

Warning triangles are used to alert approaching traffic that there is a vehicle breakdown or collision ahead. When you come across a warning triangle, you should slow down and be prepared to stop if necessary. Do not allow yourself to be distracted by the incident.

The driver is approaching traffic lights that they know have been green for some time. What should the driver do?

The driver should prepare to stop in case the lights change before they reach them.

You should always read the road ahead and be prepared to react to changing traffic situations.

Where traffic lights have been green for some time, you should be prepared to stop, as the lights are probably about to change to amber.

What should a driver do when approaching a junction normally controlled by traffic lights and the traffic lights are not lighting?

Treat the junction as an unmarked junction and proceed cautiously while watching out for other traffic.

You should always read the road ahead and be prepared to react to changing traffic situations.

If the traffic lights are not working, you should approach the junction with extra care, and you should proceed only when it is safe to do so.

What should the driver do if there are cattle on the road ahead?

The driver should reduce speed and overtake with care.

What should a driver do if they see horse riders on the road ahead?

The driver should reduce speed and allow extra clearance and pass with care.

You should always read the road ahead and be prepared to react to changing traffic situations.

If you meet cattle, horses or other animals on the road, you should slow down and be prepared to stop. Don't use the horn or do anything that might frighten the animals. You must stop if directed to do so by the person in charge of animals.

What should drivers be aware of if they meet horses with riders on the road?

Drivers should be aware that loud noises from their vehicle may frighten the horses and cause them to bolt.

You must know your responsibilities towards animal traffic on the road. Horses are easily startled and any sudden noises or activity could cause them to bolt.

What should the driver do when approaching a humpbacked hill?

The driver should reduce speed, keep to the left and be alert for hazards ahead.

As you approach a humpbacked bridge or hill, you should be aware that there might be hidden dangers ahead – for example, overtaking traffic coming towards you.

You should always read the road ahead and be prepared to react to changing traffic situations such as this.

What should a driver do if there is a large oil spill on the road?

Reduce speed by gently applying the brakes and switch on the hazard warning lights.

Where oil is spilt on the road, your tyres will have reduced grip, and you might be at risk of skidding if you brake sharply.

If you do come across oil on the road, brake gently and switch on your hazard warning lights for a short period to alert other traffic to the hazard.

What do flashing amber beacons on an oncoming vehicle alert a driver to?

That the oncoming vehicle may be slow moving or extra wide.

What should a driver do if they meet a vehicle with flashing amber beacons?

Slow down and prepare to stop.

Flashing amber beacons are used by recovery vehicles and vehicles carrying abnormal loads. You should be aware that these vehicles may need extra room and could conceal following traffic. When you come across such vehicles, slow down and be prepared to stop if necessary.

What should a driver be aware of before crossing railway or tram lines?

There may be an uneven surface and tyre grip may be reduced when crossing the rails.

You should be aware of the impact of changes in the road surface. For example, at railway and tram crossings the uneven surface or oil deposits could reduce the grip of your tyres.

Slow down as you approach railway or tram crossings and increase your distance from the vehicle in front.

What should the driver be aware of when crossing road markings such as lines and directional arrows?

The stopping distance is increased due to reduced tyre grip.

You should be aware of the impact of changes in the road surface. For example, road markings and directional arrows can become slippery when wet. Where possible, avoid driving on road markings, and be aware of the increased risk of skidding.

Consideration for other road users

While driving, you need to show consideration for other road users at all times.

There are pedestrians on the footpath ahead and there are pools of water on the road. What should a driver do?

Reduce speed and try to avoid the pools of water so as not to splash the pedestrians.

During wet conditions, you should be aware that surface water can affect the stability of your vehicle. This is particularly so where the water lies in pools. As you drive through surface water, you should show consideration to pedestrians and cyclists and try not to splash them as you pass.

When preparing to stop, a driver notices the vehicle behind is towing a trailer. What should the driver do?

Indicate in good time and pull in gradually to allow the vehicle behind extra stopping distance.

When you are slowing down or stopping, you should be mindful of the type of vehicle that is following you. For example, if the vehicle following you is a large vehicle or one towing a trailer, you should think of indicating a little earlier than normal to allow the following vehicle enough time to react safely.

The bus ahead is moving away from a bus stop. What should a driver do?

Slow down and allow it to move out.

A driver should allow signalling buses back into the stream of traffic when they are moving out from a stop. Be careful of pedestrians getting on and off buses, particularly of children near schools.

What should a driver do on a narrow road when another vehicle is coming in the opposite direction?

Reduce speed and allow reasonable clearance between their vehicle and the oncoming one before proceeding.

You should always be prepared to react to hazards ahead. When you meet a vehicle coming against you on a narrow road, you should show consideration and slow down to a appropriate speed so that the two vehicles can pass each other safely.

When driving along and wishing to stop at a shop on the side of the street in order to make a purchase, what should a driver do?

Continue on to a safe parking space.

You may park only where it is safe and legal to do so. Your parked vehicle must not cause a danger or an obstruction to other road users.

When a driver is driving behind another vehicle that they do not intend to overtake, what should the driver do?

Keep well back to allow following traffic to overtake them.

You should always allow sufficient distance between your vehicle and the vehicle in front. This will enable you to stop safely if necessary, and it will give overtaking vehicles enough room to pull in safely to the left lane after they have passed you.

Why is tailgating (driving too close behind the vehicle in front) dangerous?

The vehicle will not have sufficient distance to stop safely in an emergency.

Is tailgating allowed on a motorway or dual carriageway?

No, because the vehicle in front may stop suddenly.

If you drive too close to the vehicle in front and it brakes suddenly, you will not have enough time to react. For that reason you should always keep a safe distance from the vehicle in front.

One way of calculating a safe distance is the 'two-second rule': allow at least two seconds to elapse between the vehicle in front and your own vehicle passing a fixed point such as a lamp post or sign post.

Alertness to danger

Dangerous situations can arise without warning, so you need to be alert at all times to changing road and traffic situations.

What danger can arise during daylight when a driver enters an area that is heavily shaded by overhanging trees?

Visibility could be suddenly reduced.

When you enter a heavily shaded area after driving in bright sunlight, it might take a while for your eyes to adjust to the change, and you might not see a hazard immediately ahead.

What should a driver do when being overtaken by another vehicle?

Continue at the same pace.

When you are being overtaken by another vehicle, you should continue at the same pace but be alert in case the overtaking vehicle suddenly pulls back in front you.

When should signals (for example, with indicators) be given to other road users?

Clearly and in good time to let other road users know your intentions.

How does giving a late signal affect other road users?

They may not have sufficient time to react.

Giving signals is a way of telling other road users what you intend to do. So, you should signal properly before moving off, turning right or left, changing lanes, overtaking, slowing down or stopping. Signal clearly and in good time, and keep in mind that giving a signal does not give you the right of way. Late signals may confuse other road users.

When driving into a narrow gap between oncoming vehicles and vehicles parked on the left. What should a driver do?

Indicate right, stopping if necessary until oncoming traffic has passed by.

When you meet approaching traffic at a narrow gap, you should show consideration and slow down to a appropriate speed so that you and the other vehicles can pass each other safely. If necessary, give way to the other vehicles.

Observation and field of view

When you are driving, you must always have a clear picture of the road ahead and the traffic conditions all around you. You should also make sure that other road users can see you, so that they are not taken by surprise and forced to take emergency evasive action.

Visibility

The questions in this section deal with situations where your ability to see the road ahead is restricted and with the effects of rain on your ability to control your vehicle.

How does rain affect driving in this situation?

It increases the danger of skidding.

When it is wet, your tyres do not grip the road surface as well as when it is dry, your stopping distance is increased and you are more likely to skid. For these reasons you should slow down during or after rain and keep a greater distance from the vehicle in front.

When a driver is at a junction where visibility is extremely limited, what should the driver do?

Move out with extreme care, watching carefully to the left and right.

Where your view is obstructed at a junction, you should move carefully into a position where you can see, but without interfering with other road users. You should then assess the situation before you continue.

When should a driver use the vehicle's rear view mirror?

Before changing direction.

You should use your mirrors to stay aware of traffic situations behind and around you. Always check your mirror before you change direction on a road, and before you signal or begin a manoeuvre.

How should a driver proceed if their view is obstructed at a junction?

Move out slowly onto the road while watching carefully for other traffic.

At junctions where the view is obstructed, move carefully into a position where you can see without interfering with other road users. Then assess the situation before you continue.

What should a driver do when approaching traffic lights that are stuck on red?

Stop and proceed with great caution.

When you approach a junction with the traffic lights stuck on red, stop at the line, take the required observation and proceed with caution when it is safe to do so. Treat the junction as 'unmarked' and do not assume that you have the right of way.

What should a driver do when there are dark clouds and visibility is reduced during daylight hours?

Drive with side-lights or dipped headlights switched on.

Drivers need to see and be seen during all periods of low light levels – for example, at dusk and dawn and in some bad weather conditions. At times of low light, you should turn on dipped headlights.

The Road Safety Authority recommends that motorcyclists and drivers turn on their dipped headlights or daytime running lights during daylight hours.

Blindspots

When driving, you need to be aware of the fact that there are some parts of the road around you that you cannot see easily, either directly or with your mirrors. You need to be sure that these areas are clear of other road users before moving into them. Equally, when travelling behind a truck or other large vehicle, or when overtaking another vehicle, you should be aware that there are times when you are 'invisible' to the other driver.

When driving behind a heavy goods vehicle that is signalling to turn right, what should a driver do?

Stay behind until there is sufficient space to overtake it on the inside or until it has completed the turn.

Heavy goods vehicles need extra space on the road, and when they are turning the overhang of the vehicle may swing out into the path of overtaking or passing traffic. For that reason, it is a good idea to stay back and let the heavy goods vehicle complete its turn unless there is sufficient space to overtake safely.

When driving behind a bus that is signalling to turn left and there is oncoming traffic, what should a driver do?

Stay back and allow it to complete the turn.

Before you overtake another vehicle, you should make sure that the road ahead is clear (with no oncoming traffic) and that you can get back to your own side of the road without interfering with the path or progress of other road users.

Always allow a bus to complete a left hand turn – this is because your field of view might be restricted and it could be dangerous to attempt overtaking it.

What should a driver do when driving on a wide road behind a vehicle that has signalled to turn right ahead?

Overtake on the left-hand side and carry on.

You may overtake on the left when the driver in front has moved out and signalled their intent to turn right and you are going straight ahead – provided there is enough room to do so safely and your path will not be obstructed by the swing of a large vehicle turning right.

What might be described as a bus driver's 'blind spots'?

The areas to the front, sides and rear of the bus which the driver cannot see.

Where are the blind spots on a truck (for its driver) that a driver in a car behind the truck needs to be aware of?

The areas to the front, sides and rear which the driver of the truck cannot see.

Where are the blind spots that a driver needs to be aware of when towing a loaded trailer?

The area to the side and rear of the vehicle and of the trailer that the driver cannot see.

A blind spot is an area a driver cannot see when looking forward or when looking in the mirrors. You should always check your blindspots before changing direction.

Overtaking and U-turns

The questions that follow deal with overtaking on the left and performing U-turns. Each of these manoeuvres can be done only in limited circumstances; they each require the driver to exercise judgement and skill.

When is it permissible to overtake another vehicle on the left-hand side?

When the vehicle in front is signalling to turn right.

You may overtake on the left when the driver in front has moved out and signalled their intent to turn right and you are going straight ahead – provided there is enough room to do so safely and your path will not be obstructed by the swing of a large vehicle turning right.

What should a driver who wishes to perform a U-turn do?

Check ahead and behind for approaching traffic.

If you want to do a U-turn you must first choose a place where it is safe and legal to do it. Check all around for other road users and do not impede their right of way. Complete the manoeuvre efficiently and safely.

What should a driver who wishes to perform a turnabout do?

Check ahead and behind for oncoming traffic and turn briskly while still keeping a look out.

> If you want to do a turnabout, you must first choose a place where it is safe and legal to do so. Check all around for other road users and do not impede their right of way. Complete the manoeuvre efficiently and safely.

The driver's mental state

Driving a motor vehicle requires concentration, perception, judgement and reaction. These can all be affected if your mental state is impaired by tiredness, by being under pressure, by anger or distress, by frustrating or confusing traffic conditions, or by alcohol or drugs. The questions in this section check that you understand these issues and know how to deal with them.

Tiredness

Tiredness – or fatigue – is one of the main causes of serious road collisions. When you're very tired, you are much less alert and have poorer physical coordination, and your reaction times are much slower. You will also find it more difficult to 'read the road' and take in direction signs, warning signs and other information as you drive. And you run the very grave risk of dozing off at the wheel, with potentially fatal consequences.

What should drivers do if they become drowsy while driving?

Stop, take a break including a short walk if possible.

What should the driver do if they are driving and feel tired?

The driver should stop and take a break.

> Driving when you are tired can be very dangerous, and tiredness is one of the main causes of serious road collisions. Being very tired may cause you to micro-sleep (or nod off momentarily). At 100km/h you travel at 28 metres a second, so if you micro-sleep for just 4 seconds you would travel over 100 metres without being in control of the vehicle.
>
> Never drive if you are fighting sleep. If you do become drowsy while driving, stop in a safe place and take a short nap. Then get some fresh air and stretch your legs for a few minutes before setting off again. Taking a caffeine-based drink such as coffee may also help.

Resisting pressure

There are so many things that can stress you when you are driving: heavy traffic, bad weather, road works, waiting at level crossings, other drivers' bad behaviour – all of these can build up frustration and make it difficult to stay calm and focus on arriving safely at your destination. Your own emotional state can also play a big part in how well you drive. If you are worried or upset, angry or depressed, it will probably show in your driving.

What should a driver do if they are behind schedule in reaching a destination at an appointed time?

Be patient and drive so as to arrive safely.

You should always drive at a speed that allows you to stop safely within the distance you can see to be clear.

Being late for an appointment is no excuse for exceeding speed limits or for driving at an unsafe speed. Arrive alive.

What should a driver do if they do not want to travel as fast as the vehicle in front?

The driver should keep to the left and allow vehicles to overtake if they wish.

Always read the road ahead and be prepared to react to any traffic situation. You should not drive so slowly that your vehicle unnecessarily blocks other road users. If you want to allow a vehicle behind to overtake, you may pull into the hard shoulder briefly as long as no pedestrians or cyclists are using it and there are no junctions or entrances nearby.

What should a driver do if they wish to drive across a busy road and the traffic lights that normally control the junction are temporarily out of action?

Take good observation, wait for a clear break in the traffic and proceed to cross the road.

Always read the road ahead and be prepared to react to any traffic situation. In this case, do not proceed until it is clear and safe to do so. Do not assume that you have the right of way.

What should a driver do if they see a school bus stopped on the left-hand side of the road ahead?

Reduce speed and overtake with caution.

Always read the road and be prepared to react to any traffic situation – in this case, be aware of vulnerable road users such as school children boarding or alighting from school buses.

What should the driver do when driving behind a vehicle that is going from side to side on the road in an unsafe manner?

The driver should stay well back until the road widens sufficiently to allow safe overtaking.

You should always be prepared to react to hazards ahead. If the vehicle in front is moving from side to side, it may indicate that the driver is not paying full attention or that their driving is impaired by drink, drugs or tiredness.

Overtake such a vehicle only if you are sure it is safe to do so. If you think the vehicle is a risk to the public safety, you should report it to the Gardaí or to traffic watch lo-call 1890 205 805.

What should a driver do if a heavy goods vehicle in front has moved out to make a left turn ahead?

Stay behind it and allow it to finish the turn.

What should a driver do if a bus in front has moved out to make a left-hand turn and there is oncoming traffic?

Stay back and allow the bus to complete the turn.

Always read the road ahead and be prepared to react to any traffic situation. In this case, you should be aware that the larger vehicle will need extra space to complete the left-hand turn, and you should remain behind it until it has completed its turn.

What should a driver do if they see a truck reversing into a side entrance on the left-hand side of the road ahead?

Stop and wait until the way is clear.

Always read the road ahead and be prepared to react to any traffic situation. You should be aware of the difficulties that drivers of large vehicles can have reversing into a side entrance.

In this case, a large vehicle reversing could obstruct your view of the road ahead as you approach, and you should proceed only if you are sure the way ahead is clear.

What should a driver do if they wish to turn right at traffic lights while the green light is showing and there is oncoming traffic approaching?

Go forward towards the centre of the junction and wait for a suitable gap to appear in the oncoming traffic before making the turn.

If you wish to turn right at a set of traffic lights, drive into the junction when you see a green light, taking care not to block any oncoming traffic. Then complete the turn when it is safe to do so.

When is it permitted to force oncoming traffic onto the hard shoulder on the opposite side of the road while overtaking?

It is not permitted to force oncoming traffic onto the hard shoulder while overtaking.

Forcing oncoming traffic onto the hard shoulder on the opposite side of the road – is this safe driving?

No, this is dangerous driving.

Overtaking in the manner described here is dangerous. You should overtake another vehicle only when it is safe to do so, both for you and for all other traffic.

Before you overtake, make sure the road ahead is clear and that you have enough room to complete the overtaking manoeuvre and return to your own side of the road without forcing any other road user to alter speed or course.

When meeting oncoming traffic on a national road, is it permitted to move into the hard shoulder to allow following traffic to overtake?

When driving on a national road is it permitted to drive on the hard shoulder in order to allow faster-moving traffic to overtake?

Yes, temporarily when the hard shoulder is clear and it is safe to drive there while the traffic is overtaking.

On national roads, the hard shoulder is normally for the use of pedestrians and cyclists only. If you want to allow a vehicle behind to overtake, you may pull into the hard shoulder briefly as long as no pedestrians or cyclists are using it and there are no junctions or entrances nearby.

In the case of motorways, however, you must not drive on the hard shoulder, except in an emergency.

What action should a driver take in a queue of traffic controlled by traffic lights?

A driver should always maintain their position in the queue.

Always read the road ahead and be prepared to react to any traffic situation. From time to time you may have to queue in traffic. In this situation, you should try to remain patient and considerate of other road users. Jumping the queue is inconsiderate, it could be dangerous , and may it could even provoke a road rage incident or cause a collision.

What should the driver do when driving a vehicle they are not familiar with?

Drive initially with extra care and at a lower speed than normal.

You should know where to find and how to operate all the controls on your vehicle, including all of its safety features and warning lamps. When you are driving, you need to be able to concentrate on what's happening around you and operating the vehicle controls should be second nature to you.

When you sit into the driver's seat of a vehicle you are not familiar with, you should do a thorough 'cockpit drill' before you move off.

What should drivers do if they approach road works and there is earth-moving machinery moving about?

Reduce speed as there may be loose gravel or mud on the road.

Where earth-moving machinery is working, there are likely to be mud and gravel deposits on the road. Also the noise of such machines might make it hard for road workers to hear the approaching traffic. When you come across earth-moving machinery, slow down and proceed with extreme caution.

Subject to the speed limit, what is the 'safest' speed to drive at?

The speed that will enable the driver to stop the vehicle within the distance ahead that they can see to be clear.

You should always drive at a speed that allows you to stop within the distance ahead that you can see to be clear.

If you don't think you could safely bring the vehicle to a stop within the range of what you can see, then you're driving too fast – slow down.

Keeping full attention on the road

When you are driving you need to take in a great deal of information – about other traffic, road conditions, direction and warning signs, and so on. Just dealing with that amount of information is quite enough, and you don't need to add to the load by letting yourself be distracted. When you are distracted, your reactions are slower and your judgement is not as good. Remember that it is an offence to drive 'without due care and attention'.

When driving along and wishing to use a hand-held mobile phone, what should a driver do?

Stop at a safe location before using the phone.

It is an offence and very unsafe to use a hand-held mobile phone while driving a vehicle or riding a motorbike. It is unsafe because it prevents you from concentrating fully on your driving.

Using a hands-free phone kit is not illegal, but in some circumstances it could be a dangerous distraction, and you could be prosecuted for dangerous driving, careless driving or driving without due care and attention.

When stopped at traffic lights and the green light comes on, what should a driver do?

Check that other road users have cleared the junction and move off with care.

When stopped at traffic lights and the green light comes on, you should check to ensure the way is clear and proceed only if it is safe to do so.

Patience and courtesy

Aggressive and impatient behaviour can very easily turn into 'road rage', where people who are normally civil and courteous lose self-control and act very irresponsibly. Don't allow yourself to be provoked by other drivers' bad behaviour. Let such drivers go ahead – you will be safer if you are not in their vicinity.

Good drivers stay patient, courteous and tolerant at all times and don't respond to provocation – they know that they'll get there just as quickly if they ignore such actions.

What should a driver do if another vehicle blocks their right of way at a junction?

Be patient.

You should always try to show restraint. It is important to understand that the right of way is not an absolute right of way, and you must always proceed with caution and with regard for other road users.

A driver who is about to undertake a journey is upset or angry. What should they do?

Not drive until they are calm.

If you drive when you are angry or upset, you are more likely to be involved in a collision, and more likely to react to other drivers' bad behaviour. Take the time to calm down and compose yourself before you set out on a journey.

When being overtaken and there is oncoming traffic, what should a driver do?

Reduce speed and allow the overtaking vehicle to return the left side of the road after completing the overtaking manoeuvre.

When you are being overtaken and there are oncoming vehicles, you should show consideration for all the other traffic and slow down to allow the overtaking vehicle to move in front of you to avoid the risk of a collision.

When in a hurry and another vehicle cuts in front, what should a driver do?

Be patient and not retaliate.

If another driver behaves badly, you should try not let it annoy you – show restraint and don't react. Road rage only increases the risk of a collision.

What should a driver do when they get a puncture while driving?

Stop at a safe place and change the tyre.

If you get a puncture while driving, find a suitable and safe place to stop and change the wheel. If you can't find a suitable place immediately, drive slowly (with your hazard warning lights turned on) to avoid further damage to the tyre or rim until a safe place is found.

What should a driver do when they want to change to the lane on the right in which there is other traffic?

Use the mirror, signal and move into the right-hand lane when a suitable gap appears in the traffic in that lane.

Any time you change lanes, you should use the Mirror–Signal–Mirror (blind spots)–Manoeuvre routine.

Check your mirrors, signal your intention, check your mirrors again (and your blind spots), and when a suitable gap becomes available manoeuvre the vehicle into the next lane, giving way to traffic already in that lane.

Alcohol and drugs

Alcohol and many other drugs seriously impair your ability to drive safely. The questions in this section check that you fully understand this issue and know how to comply with the law in this respect.

What effect does alcohol have on driver behaviour?

It slows down a driver's reactions.

It makes the driver drowsy.

Alcohol is a major factor in collisions that lead to death and injury. Even small amounts of alcohol affect your judgement, your concentration and your ability to react to hazards. A driver should never ever drink and drive.

If a motorist or a motorcyclist is taking medication which may affect their driving, what should they do?

Seek medical advice in relation to driving.

If taking unprescribed medication what should a driver check before driving their vehicle?

Check that the medication does not affect driving.

Some medication can affect a driver's ability to drive safely.

If you are on medication of any kind, you should ask your doctor or pharmacist to tell you if it is safe to drive while taking it. Read the patient information leaflet supplied with the medication.

Overtaking and driving when weather or road conditions are hazardous

Before overtaking a slower-moving vehicle, ask yourself whether it is necessary to do so, whether it is legal, and, above all, whether it is safe. When passing parked vehicles, leave enough room for the door of the parked vehicle to open. And when driving on icy roads, make sure that you leave enough stopping distance between your vehicle and the vehicle in front.

What effect does a wet road surface have on a vehicle's braking ability?

Generally, it doubles the normal braking distance required on a dry surface.

When it is wet, your tyres do not grip the road surface as well as when it is dry and your stopping distance is increased. For these reasons you should slow down during or after rain and keep a greater distance from the vehicle in front.

When driving uphill behind a slow-moving vehicle, what should a driver do?

Stay well behind the vehicle until it can be overtaken safely.

Overtake only if your view of the road ahead is completely clear, there is no oncoming traffic and you can complete the manoeuvre safely.

Do not overtake when you are approaching the brow of a hill where you cannot see if there is oncoming traffic.

After overtaking another vehicle, what should a driver do?

Gradually move back into the left when the vehicle has been overtaken.

After overtaking, check your mirrors, signal and return to your normal lane position as soon as it is safe. Take a smooth easy line and don't cut in sharply.

What could happen if a driver cuts in too soon when overtaking another vehicle?

Both vehicles could collide.

You should always ensure that you are safely past the vehicle you are overtaking before resuming normal lane position. Cutting in too soon could lead to a collision.

What should a driver do when overtaking parked vehicles?

Allow sufficient clearance when passing.

What clearance should drivers normally allow for parked vehicles?

A door width.

When you are passing a parked vehicle, move into the correct position in good time and leave plenty of clearance room between your vehicle and the parked vehicle – just in case someone opens the door in front of you.

What stopping distance should a driver allow when they suspect that the road might be icy?

Up to ten times the normal distance.

When driving in snow or icy conditions a driver should allow a much greater distance from the vehicle in front, as stopping distances can be increased by up to ten times the normal.

Roadholding

Your ability to control your vehicle and to stop it safely and effectively depends to a large extent on the quality of your tyres, the road surface and the contact between them. The tyres' grip on the road can be reduced or even eliminated by water, oil, ice, wet leaves, or loose chippings. You need to be aware of this fact, and reduce speed if you are driving in these conditions.

Why does it take longer to stop the vehicle after heavy rain?

The tyres have less road grip than in dry weather.

When it is wet, your tyres do not grip the road surface as well as when it is dry and your stopping distance is increased. For these reasons you should slow down during or after rain and keep a greater distance from the vehicle in front.

What is the effect on driving if there is a film of water between the vehicle's tyres and the road surface?

Steering and braking will be less effective.

On a wet road, a film of water can build up between the tyres and the road surface. This is called 'aquaplaning ' and it has the effect of reducing the grip of the tyres on the road.

What should a driver do if they encounter loose chippings on a road?

Slow down and allow extra clearance to all traffic until they have gone past the area with the loose chippings.

Where there are loose chippings on the road, you should slow down and leave extra room (or clearance) between your vehicle and other traffic. This will also give you more time to stop if you need to, and it will help to reduce the amount of chippings your vehicle throws up against other vehicles.

What effect does spilt diesel have on a road?

It makes the road more slippery.

Diesel spilt on the road can make the road surface extremely slippery, particularly if the road is wet.

What should a driver do when driving in slippery road conditions?

Drive at lower speeds and use gentle acceleration and braking.

When driving in slippery road conditions, you should be particularly smooth and gradual in the way you accelerate and brake. This will help you avoid skidding or slipping.

What should a driver do when travelling downhill on snow or ice?

Use an appropriate lower gear and brake gently to reduce speed.

When travelling downhill in snow or ice, you should select a lower gear to take advantage of engine braking and use the brakes very gently when you need to.

Maintaining a safe distance from the vehicle in front

Never drive too close to the vehicle in front of you. The faster the traffic is moving, the greater the distance you should allow. The distance it will take you to stop in an emergency depends on many things, including how alert you are, the type and condition of the road surface, and the condition of your brakes and tyres. The questions in this section check that you understand the need to keep your distance, and that you know how to do so.

How does driving at high speed affect a vehicle's road holding?

The road holding ability of the vehicle is reduced.

Driving at high speed is a factor that affects road holding. At higher speeds the airflow under a vehicle reduces tyre grip on the road and when you are approaching a bend or corner, the momentum of the vehicle makes it more difficult to change direction.

What is the minimum safe distance to leave between vehicles travelling at 100km/h on a dry road?

62 metres.

The figure of 62 metres is based on the two-second rule. If you follow the two-second rule, you will leave approximately 1 metre between you and the vehicle in front for every 1.6km/h of your speed.

What is a likely consequence of sudden braking?

The vehicle could be hit from behind.

As well as reading the road ahead, you should also be aware of traffic coming behind you. This will help you react correctly in a situation where you need to brake suddenly.

What affects the braking distance of a vehicle?

The speed and weight of the vehicle.

The overall stopping distance of your vehicle depends on its speed and weight. Faster and heavier vehicles require greater stopping distances.

What is the normal stopping distance of a car or motorcycle travelling at 50km/h on a dry road?

24 metres.

What is the normal stopping distance of a car or motorcycle travelling at 50km/h on a wet road?

35 metres.

What is the normal stopping distance of a car or motorcycle travelling a 100km/h on a dry road?

77 metres.

What is the normal stopping distance of a car or motorcycle travelling at 100km/h on a wet road?

122 metres.

Normal stopping distance is the distance you travel while you react to a situation *plus* the distance you travel while you are bringing the vehicle to a stop.

On a wet road, it will take longer to bring the vehicle to a stop, as the tyres do not grip the road as well in the wet.

In dry weather how might a driver judge what is a safe following distance from the vehicle in front?

By allowing at least two seconds to elapse between the vehicle in front and the driver's own vehicle passing a fixed point.

You should maintain a gap of at least two seconds from the vehicle in front – that's the two-second rule.

In wet weather how might a driver judge what is a safe following distance from the vehicle in front?

By allowing at least four seconds to elapse between the vehicle in front and the driver's own vehicle passing a fixed point.

In wet conditions you should maintain a gap of at least four seconds from the vehicle in front – twice as long as in dry conditions.

What phrase is recommended for drivers to help them determine a safe following distance from the vehicle in front on a dry road?

'Only a fool breaks the two-second rule.'

You should maintain a gap of least two seconds from the vehicle in front – that's the two-second rule.

What effect does carrying a load have on a vehicle's braking ability?

It increases the distance required to stop.

When driving a vehicle which is carrying a load, the driver should be aware that the forces acting on the load under braking will increase the distance required to stop.

What effect does towing a loaded trailer have on stopping ability?

It significantly increases stopping distance.

If you are towing a loaded trailer, you need to be aware that your braking distance could be considerably greater, depending on the weight and size of the trailer.

Driving when visibility is reduced

When your visibility is reduced, such as in rain, snow or fog, you must modify your driving behaviour. The questions in this section check that you understand this issue and can take appropriate action when necessary.

What should a driver do when overtaking a large vehicle that is throwing up spray?

Move out earlier than normal and give extra clearance.

In wet weather vehicles throw up spray and muck from the road.

If you are overtaking a large vehicle in wet conditions, you need to move out earlier than normal and give yourself some extra clearance room. This will help reduce the amount of spray on your windscreen.

Drive with dipped headlights and fog lights.

Reduce speed and use dipped headlights.

In dense fog you should reduce your speed and use dipped headlights and fog lights (where fitted). Sidelights are not strong enough in fog, and full headlights can reflect off the fog and make it harder to see where you are going.

Driving at night

Driving at night is considerably more challenging than driving during the day. You need to drive more slowly to take account of the reduced visibility, and you need to use your lights to make sure that you can be seen by other road users and that you can see the road ahead.

When driving at night the full headlights should enable the driver to see for a distance of how many metres?

100 metres.

At night in good driving conditions the full headlights of a car will typically let you see 100 metres ahead. So, you should travel at a speed that allows you to stop within that distance.

When driving at night the dipped headlights should enable the driver to see for a distance of how many metres?

30 metres.

When driving at night in good driving conditions the dipped headlights of a car will typically let you see 30 metres ahead. So, you should travel at a speed that allows you to stop in that distance.

What effect could incorrectly adjusted headlights have?

Oncoming road users could be dazzled.

You are responsible for making sure that your vehicle is roadworthy and that its headlights are adjusted correctly. If the headlights are out of line they are less effective and may dazzle oncoming traffic, even when dipped.

When driving at night, when must a driver dip the vehicle's full headlights?

When must a driver use dipped headlights?

When meeting or driving behind other traffic.

What lights should a driver have on when driving close behind other traffic at night?

Dipped headlights.

> When driving at night you should dip your headlights when you meet oncoming vehicles so that you do not dazzle them.
>
> And you should also dip your headlights when you are driving behind another vehicle so the driver is not dazzled by your lights in their mirror.

A driver has been driving regularly in daylight and must now undertake a journey at night. What should the driver do?

Drive at a slower speed than in the day as visibility is reduced at night.

> If you are not very used to driving at night time, it can take quite a while to adjust to conditions at night. For that reason, you might need to drive slower until you get used to the reduced visibility at night.

What should a driver do when driving at night?

Drive at a speed that enables the driver to stop within the distance ahead that they can see to be clear.

> When driving at night in good driving conditions the full headlights of a car will typically let you see 100 metres ahead. So, you should travel at a speed that allows you to stop in that distance.

When driving at night, what is the safest approach for a driver to adopt?

Drive at a speed that enables the driver to stop within the distance ahead that they can see to be clear.

> When driving at night in good driving conditions the dipped headlights of a car will typically let you see 30 metres ahead. So, you should travel at a speed that allows you to stop in that distance.

When meeting an oncoming vehicle at night, what should a driver do?

Not look directly at the oncoming vehicle's lights.

What should a driver do if dazzled (or blinded) by the lights of an oncoming vehicle at night?

Do not look directly at the lights.

Look away and slow down and stop if necessary.

If you are dazzled by the lights of an oncoming vehicle, look towards the verge until the vehicle has passed. Slow down and stop if necessary.

When may a driver use full headlights when driving at night?

When there is no oncoming traffic.

You should use full headlights when driving at night in unlit rural areas – this will enable you to see as far ahead as possible. Make sure, however, that your lights do not dazzle or inconvenience other road users in any way.

When driving late at night what should a driver be aware of?

That there is a danger of falling asleep.

Driving when you are tired can be very dangerous, and tiredness is one of the main causes of serious road collisions.

If you become drowsy while driving, stop in a safe place and take a short nap. Then get some fresh air and stretch your legs for a few minutes before setting off again. Taking a caffeine-based drink such as coffee may also help.

When driving at night, a single headlight approaches from ahead. What should a driver do?

Be aware it may be a four-wheeled vehicle.

When you see a single oncoming headlight at night, you need to be aware that it might not be a motorcycle – it could be a car or a van with a broken headlight.

Driving on slippery roads

Driving on a road that is covered with water, oil, ice, wet leaves or loose chippings is particularly dangerous, because your vehicle's tyres have greatly reduced 'grip' on the road surface and you may skid and lose control of the vehicle. The questions in this section check that you understand this danger and know how to respond.

When is black ice likely to occur on the road?

In cold weather after rain.

Black ice occurs when moisture freezes on a very cold surface. Exposed roads and bridges can have black ice when other sections of the same road may be clear. Black ice is virtually invisible, and so presents a particular hazard for motorcyclists and drivers. In wintry conditions, if you notice a reduction in tyre noise or if the steering becomes lighter, you should suspect that there may be black ice on the road.

How might a driver know if there is black ice on the road?

There will be a decrease in road noise in the vehicle.

Steering will seem lighter.

What should a driver do if there is black ice on the road?

Avoid harsh braking, steering and acceleration.

One of the signs that you might be driving on black ice is a sudden decrease in the level of road noise. This is due to the lack of grip between the tyres and the road. Another sign is that the steering will seem lighter than normal.

If you suspect you are driving on black ice, you should avoid harsh braking, steering and acceleration. This will help reduce the risk of skidding.

What is the safest practice when driving on icy roads?

Drive at a slower speed than usual using gentle acceleration and braking.

When driving on icy roads you should avoid harsh braking, steering and acceleration. This will help reduce the risk of skidding.

When driving a vehicle, what effect could icy roads have?

The vehicle could skid more easily than normal.

Icy roads can have a dramatic effect on the way a vehicle handles, and there can be an increased risk of skidding. When driving on icy roads you should avoid harsh braking, steering and acceleration. This will help reduce the risk of skidding.

What should a driver do when driving in slippery road conditions?

Use gentle acceleration and braking.

Your tyres have less grip on the road when it is wet or icy. Slow down in slippery conditions, and keep a greater distance from the vehicle in front.

How should a driver negotiate a bend when the road is slippery?

Drive slowly and smoothly.

Be extra careful when negotiating bends in slippery conditions. Slow down gently on the approach, select the appropriate gear for the speed of the vehicle and use gentle steering and acceleration to drive around the bend. Avoid braking in the bend as this may cause the vehicle to become unstable and cause a skid.

Apart from the risk of skidding, what danger may arise when driving in snow?

Road signs and road markings may become obscured.

Road signs and road markings may become obscured by snow. If this happens you may have difficulty reading regulatory, warning and information signs. This is the main reason why these signs are different shapes. Drivers should pay particular attention when travelling in these conditions.

What should a driver do when driving in heavy rain?

Be on the alert for aquaplaning.

On a wet road, a film of water can build up between the tyres and the road surface. This is called 'aquaplaning' and it has the effect of reducing the grip of the tyres on the road, and this affects your steering and braking.

For these reasons you should slow down during and after rain and keep a greater distance from the vehicle in front.

What is the danger in driving with badly worn tyres at high speed on wet roads?

Control of the vehicle is reduced because it is gliding on a film of water.

Worn tyres will reduce a vehicle's grip on the road. This becomes more noticeable on wet roads. As tyres become worn their ability to channel away the water between the tyre and the road diminishes. The minimum legal tread depth for motorcycles is 1mm and 1.6mm for other vehicles. However tyres should be replaced before they become this worn.

What should a driver do when they encounter mud on the road?

Reduce speed and be aware of the farm or works vehicles on the road.

Where there is mud on the road you should slow down and be aware that there is a danger of skidding. Your stopping distance will also be greater where there is mud on the road.

What should a driver be aware of when crossing tram lines at an angle?

Be aware that tyre grip is reduced on the lines.

Tyre grip may be reduced when you cross tram lines, especially in icy or wet conditions. As you approach tram lines, you should slow down, avoid harsh acceleration or sudden braking, and keep a greater distance from the vehicle in front. Be extra careful when there are vulnerable road users such as pedestrians and cyclists using the crossing.

What should a driver be aware of when crossing road markings such as lines or arrows?

Tyre grip is reduced.

Tyre grip is reduced when you are crossing road markings such as arrows and lines, and you should be extra careful when driving over these in wet conditions.

Driving on flooded roads

When you have driven through a large puddle or flooded area, you should test your brakes to make sure that they have not been affected by the water. If they have been affected (and if it is safe to do so), press gently on the brake pedal as you are driving until the brakes dry out and return to normal.

What should a driver do after passing through a flooded section of road?

Apply the brake pedal lightly at slow speed for a short distance to dry the brakes.

When you drive through a flooded section of road, your brakes may become less effective. If this happens, test your brakes to ensure that they have not been affected by the water – check in your mirrors before you do this. If they have been affected (and this is more than likely just temporary), press gently on the brake pedal as you are driving until they dry out and return to normal.

How does wet weather affect a vehicle's engine performance?

It has no effect on power output.

Wet weather does not affect the performance of the vehicle's engine. It does, however, affect the vehicle's road holding and braking distances. It can also affect a driver's observations.

What should a driver do where a section of road ahead has a shallow flooded area?

Reduce speed and use a lower gear.

When you approach a stretch of road with shallow flooding, you should reduce your speed and assess the area for any danger. As you drive through surface water, you should think of pedestrians and cyclists and try not to splash them as you pass.

Roadworks

The National Roads Authority and local authorities around the country are continually working to provide a safe, efficient road network and to maintain the quality of road surfaces. Roadworks include the construction of new roads, emergency repairs, routine maintenance of fences and barriers, trimming hedgerows, clearing litter, cutting grass verges, and so on.

When you come across roadworks of any kind, you need to drive with extra care, for your own safety, the safety of other road users and the safety of the road workers.

What should a driver do when they approach roadworks warning signs?

Reduce speed and be prepared to stop for works vehicles or a flagman.

You should always approach roadworks with caution as there are many possible hazards to deal with – including road workers, works vehicles, uneven road surfaces and temporary traffic controls.

What should a driver be aware of when driving through a section of road where roadworks are ongoing?

That the surface may be slippery due to mud or loose chippings.

When you are travelling through a section of roadworks, you need to be extra careful, as the road surface may be uneven or slippery or there may be loose chippings, all of which can affect road holding.

Driving on different types of road

Different types of road require you to drive in different ways, impose different restrictions on what you must or must not do, and present different things that you must look out for. The questions in this section deal with a variety of road types and the challenges they present, and check that you know how to behave when driving on them.

One-way streets

Driving on a one-way street can be confusing. Your inclination may be to always adopt a position to the left of the street, as would be appropriate if it were a two-way street. However, if you wish to turn right off the street, you should take up a position to the right.

When driving on a one-way street and wishing to turn right, what should a driver do?

Drive close to the right-hand side of the road.

Move to the right-hand side in good time.

> When driving on a one-way street, you should normally keep to the left. When you want to turn right, you should check your mirrors, signal right and manoeuvre into the right-hand side when it is safe to do so. Then complete the turn into the appropriate lane of the street you are entering.

Bus lanes

There are two types of bus lane: 'with-flow' bus lanes and 'contra-flow' bus lanes, and the rules governing what vehicles may use them are different. In addition, a bus lane may be operational only at certain times of the day, as specified on the plate accompanying the bus lane sign.

When may a driver drive in a contra-flow bus lane?

When driving a bus on a scheduled service.

What traffic may use a contra-flow bus lane?

Buses on a scheduled service.

What traffic may use a with-flow bus lane during the specified times?

Buses, taxis and cyclists.

When may a driver (other than a bus or taxi driver) drive in a with-flow bus lane?

Outside the hours specified on the bus lane information plate.

A bus lane is a special lane for the use of buses. A with-flow bus lane is one that runs in the same direction as the traffic beside it. Taxis and cyclists may also use with-flow bus lanes. Other traffic may use them outside the hours posted on the accompanying plate.

A contra-flow bus lane is one that runs in the opposite direction to traffic beside it. Only buses on a scheduled service may use a contra-flow bus lane.

When a driver wants to turn left into a property and there is a bus lane on the left, what should the driver do?

Watch out for cyclists, taxis and buses which may be using the bus lane.

If you need to cross a bus lane on your left in order to enter a property, you should take extra care that there are no buses, taxis or cyclists in the bus lane. Check your mirrors, signal and turn into the property when it is safe to do so.

Dual carriageways

The questions in this section deal with entering, crossing and driving along dual carriageways. Traffic on these roads is generally faster that on other roads, so you need to know how to act appropriately without undue hesitation.

When driving along a dual carriageway, what lane position should a driver be in?

In the left-hand lane unless the driver wishes to overtake or turn right.

You must normally drive in the left-hand lane of a dual carriageway, except when overtaking or turning right a short distance ahead.

When turning right from a minor road onto a dual carriageway with a wide median strip, what should a driver do?

When clear on the right, proceed to the central median and then wait until it is clear on the left before proceeding.

> If you wish to turn right onto a dual carriageway from a minor road and the central median is big enough, you may complete the manoeuvre in two stages.
>
> 1. Wait until it is clear on the right, and proceed to the central median.
> 2. Wait in the central median until it is clear from the left, and then complete the turn.

When turning right from a minor road onto a dual carriageway with a narrow median strip, what should a driver do?

Wait on the minor road until there is a suitable gap in the traffic from both directions.

> If you wish to turn right onto a dual carriageway from a minor road and the central median is not big enough to accommodate your vehicle, you should wait on the minor road until it is clear from both sides of the road before completing the turn.

'2-plus-1' roads

'2-plus-1' roads provide two lanes in one direction and one lane in the opposite direction. On the two-lane side, it is generally safe to overtake. Approximately every two kilometres, the two-lane side is replaced by one lane and the one-lane side opens out into two lanes. The questions in this section check that you understand how to drive on such roads.

What does a 2-plus-1 road have?

Two non-motorway lanes in one direction and one non-motorway lane in the opposite direction.
Two lanes of traffic in one direction and one in the opposite direction.

On a 2-plus-1 road, where is a driver allowed to turn right?

At controlled junctions.

Where may a driver overtake on a 2-plus-1 road?

In the two-lane stretch.

A '2-plus-1' road consists of two lanes in one direction of travel and one lane in the other direction. When you need to overtake, you should wait until you reach the 2-lane section which occurs approximately every 2 kilometres.

Where there are safety barriers separating the two directions of traffic, you may turn right only at controlled junctions.

Motorways

Driving on a motorway requires concentration and discipline. You need to know exactly how to behave when entering and leaving a motorway, how to drive on it, and what to expect from other drivers while on it. Although you are not permitted to drive on a motorway while holding a learner permit, the questions in this section check that you know and understand the issues involved.

What should a driver do when travelling on a motorway or dual carriageway?

Be alert for other drivers who may suddenly change lanes or reduce speed.

Motorways and dual carriageways are designed to help traffic travel faster and more safely between destinations. Traffic conditions can change very quickly because of the speed and increased volumes of traffic and lanes, and you need to be particularly alert to other drivers changing lanes or reducing speed.

When driving on a motorway, what should a driver do?

Drive in the left-hand lane unless intending to overtake.

Be alert for other drivers who may suddenly change lane or reduce speed.

The normal 'keep left' rules apply when you are driving on a motorway – stay in the left lane unless you are overtaking.

In preparation for driving on a motorway, what changes should a driver make to tyre pressure?

The driver should ensure that tyre pressure is normal.

> You should ensure that the tyre pressure of your vehicle is correct at all times.
>
> Correct tyre pressure is especially important when travelling long distances, on motorways and at speed.

What should a driver do when joining a motorway from a slip road?

Try to match the vehicle speed to that of traffic already on the motorway and merge into it in a suitable gap.

> When joining a motorway you should try to match your speed to that of the motorway traffic and merge into it when a suitable gap appears, while yielding to traffic already on the motorway.

Is a driver permitted to pick up or set down a passenger on a motorway?

No, this is not permitted.

> Motorways are designed so that traffic can move faster and more freely.
>
> It is illegal and dangerous to stop a vehicle on any part of a motorway except in an emergency or when signalled to do so by a garda.

When driving on a motorway and wishing to turn back, what should a driver do?

Leave the motorway at the next exit and cross to the other side using the fly-over (or underpass).

What should a driver do if they drive past their intended exit by mistake?

Drive on and leave at the next exit.

> If you miss your intended exit when driving on a motorway, you should proceed to the next junction exit where you can leave the motorway and then rejoin it in the opposite direction.

What should a driver do when driving on a motorway and wishing to take a break?

Leave by the next exit and find a lay-by or suitable place to stop.

if you feel tired when you are driving on a motorway, stop at a motorway service area or leave at the next exit and find a suitable place to stop to take a break.

What should a driver do when leaving a motorway?

Comply with the speed limit on the road the driver is joining.

Obey the posted speed limit.

On exiting the motorway what should a driver do?

Be alert for oncoming and crossing traffic.

When you are leaving a motorway, enter the deceleration lane and reduce your speed.

Comply with the speed limit of the road you are entering – most likely you will be in a 2-way traffic system where you will encounter vulnerable road users, such as cyclists and pedestrians.

What is the difference between driving on a motorway and driving on other types of road?

Traffic usually travels at a higher speed on a motorway.

Motorways are designed so that traffic can move faster and more freely, without traffic lights, crossroads, level crossings and other road features that might slow down traffic.

There are also restrictions on who may use a motorway – for example L-drivers and motorcycles under 50cc are prohibited.

On a motorway, a driver wants to overtake another vehicle – what should the driver do?

Use their mirrors, signal and overtake in the right-hand lane.

When you want to overtake on a motorway, use the Mirror–Signal–Mirror (blind spots)– Manoeuvre routine.

Check your mirrors, signal your intention, check your mirrors again (and your blind spots), and complete the manoeuvre when it is safe to do so.

Pay particular attention to the speed of the traffic behind you before you move out.

When you have finished overtaking, move back into the left-hand lane smoothly.

What may the hard shoulder of a motorway be used for?

Stopping in an emergency.

There are extra dangers when driving on a motorway because of the increased volume of traffic and higher speed. For safety reasons you must not drive or stop on the hard shoulder of a motorway except in an emergency.

Junctions – roads of equal importance

A driver wishes to go straight ahead at a cross junction of equal importance – what should the driver do?

Give way to traffic approaching from the right.

At a cross junction of equal importance traffic approaching from the right has the right of way. It is important to understand that the right of way is not an absolute right. In such a situation, you should proceed with caution while showing due regard for other users of the road.

Clearways

What is a clearway?

An area where stopping and parking is not allowed during certain times.

You must not stop or park in a clearway area except outside the times stated on the information plate under the sign.

Parking on a hill

If you are parking on a hill, you should take steps to make sure that the vehicle does not roll down the hill after you have left it, and that there is no undue pressure on the handbrake.

What should a driver consider doing when parking a vehicle facing down a hill?

Angling the wheels towards the kerb.

What should a driver consider doing when parking on a two-way street facing downhill?

Turning the steering wheel towards the kerb.

When you are parking facing downhill, it is a good idea to angle the wheels towards the kerb. This will help to hold the vehicle in place and ease the pressure on the handbrake. Where possible, you should park with the flow of traffic.

What should a driver consider doing when parking a vehicle on a two-way street and facing uphill?

Turning the steering wheel to the right.

If you are parking on a two-way street facing uphill, it is a good idea to turn the steering to the right (away from the kerb). This means the kerb will help to hold the vehicle in place and reduce the pressure on the handbrake. Where possible, you should park with the flow of traffic.

Unmarked and narrow roads

You must know how to adopt the correct position when driving on an unmarked or narrow road. You need to be especially careful in these situations, as it may be difficult for you to see other road users and to be seen by them.

While driving on a primary road that is not divided by a central dividing line, what should a driver do?

Imagine there is a central line and drive on the left-hand side.

In the absence of road markings, you should take up a position far enough to the left to allow traffic to safely pass or overtake on the right but not so far to the left that you could endanger cyclists or pedestrians.

What should a driver do when approaching a sharp right-hand bend on a narrow road?

Reduce speed, keep well to the left and watch for oncoming traffic.

When approaching a bend, you should assess the severity of the bend and reduce speed in good time. On a right-hand bend the correct position is well to the left, so that you can have a better view of the road ahead. You should always be able to stop safely on your own side of the road within the distance you can see to be clear.

Roundabouts

The questions in this section check that you know how to negotiate roundabouts, and in particular that you know which lane to choose and understand that traffic already on the roundabout has right of way over someone about to enter it.

What should a driver do when approaching a roundabout?

Give way to traffic already on the roundabout.

You should always approach roundabouts with caution. Be prepared to give way to traffic already on the roundabout and to stop if necessary.

In what direction should a driver turn when entering a roundabout?

To the left.

By law you must enter a roundabout by turning to the left and giving way to traffic already on the roundabout.

Where two lanes are provided on the approach to a roundabout, which lane should a driver select when they intend taking an exit to the right of the roundabout?

The right-hand lane.

When you approach a roundabout where two lanes are provided, you should choose the most suitable one based on the exit you intend to take off the roundabout. The left lane is usually used for vehicles exiting to the left (9 o'clock) or straight ahead (12 o'clock) and the right is for vehicles exiting at any exit after 12 o'clock.

In what position should a driver approach a roundabout when intending to take the first exit to the left?

Approach in the left-hand lane and give way to traffic already on the roundabout.

When you intend to take an exit to the left off a roundabout, you should always approach the roundabout in the left lane. Approach with caution and yield to traffic already on the roundabout.

What must a driver be aware of before entering a roundabout?

The traffic to the right – how fast it's travelling and how close it is.

When you enter a roundabout, you must give way to traffic already on the roundabout approaching from your right. Do not enter a roundabout if by doing so you would force another vehicle to slow down or stop.

Turning right

Making a right-hand turn can be challenging, as it involves crossing the path of traffic coming in the opposite direction. The questions in this section check that you know how to make a right turn safely.

Where should a vehicle be positioned before turning right?

Just left of the centre of the road.

The correct position to be in before turning right is just left of the centre of the road. Where the road is wide enough, this position allows traffic coming behind you and going straight ahead to pass you safely on the left.

What should a driver do before turning right from a major road into a minor road?

Yield right of way to oncoming traffic and to pedestrians crossing at the junction.

You must yield to oncoming traffic when turning right from a major road to a minor road.

Driving in tunnels

If you are driving through a tunnel, your driving behaviour can present a hazard to yourself and to other road users. The questions in this section check that you understand how to drive in tunnels and how to respond to situations that might arise in a tunnel.

What should a driver do when entering a tunnel?

Switch on dipped headlights.

Keep a safe distance from the vehicle in front.

Remove sunglasses, if wearing them.

As you enter the tunnel, turn on your dipped headlights and if you are wearing sunglasses, take them off.

Tailgating could be particularly dangerous in a tunnel. So, while you are in the tunnel, keep a safe distance from the vehicle in front – the minimum safe distance for a car or motorcycle is 50 metres and for all other vehicles it's 100 metres.

Pay attention to any information signs displayed.

When driving through a tunnel what should a driver do?

Keep further back than normal from the vehicle in front.

While you are driving in the tunnel, keep a safe distance from the vehicle in front – the minimum safe distance for a car or motorcycle is 50 metres and for all other vehicles it's 100 metres.

What should a driver do if there is traffic congestion in a tunnel?

Switch on hazard warning lights.

If there is traffic congestion in a tunnel, you should switch on hazard lights and remain patient. Keep a safe distance from the vehicle in front even in slow-moving traffic. Listen for traffic messages on the tunnel radio station, if available.

What should a driver do if traffic comes to a halt in a tunnel?

Switch off the engine.

If traffic comes to a halt in a tunnel, switch off your engine to prevent a build up of fumes in the tunnel. Stay patient and follow the instructions of the tunnel operators.

What should a driver do if their vehicle breaks down or they are involved in a collision in a tunnel?

Switch on hazard warning lights and walk to emergency station to call for help.

Use the emergency telephone to call for help.

Switch on hazard lights and stop as close to the left-hand side as possible.

If your vehicle breaks down or is involved in a collision in a tunnel, switch on your hazard warning lights, switch off your engine, go to an emergency station and use the emergency phone to alert the tunnel operator.

What should a driver do if their vehicle goes on fire in a tunnel?

Leave the vehicle and follow the emergency escape route.

If your vehicle goes on fire in a tunnel, you should stop the vehicle as soon as possible, evacuate any passengers to a safe place, go to an emergency station and use the emergency phone to alert the tunnel operator.

Vulnerable road users

While you are driving, most of the time you will be sharing the road with other road users, including some who are particularly vulnerable, such as pedestrians, cyclists and motorcyclists, and some who are inexperienced, unskilled or careless. You need to be particularly considerate of vulnerable road users.

Patience

When good drivers meet vulnerable road users, they show patience and courtesy. It never takes much extra time, and it is safer for all concerned.

When approaching a junction where a pedestrian is crossing the road, what should a driver do?

Yield right of way to the pedestrian.

You should never put a pedestrian at risk, and you must always yield to pedestrians who have started to cross at junctions.

What should a driver do if their progress is hindered by a cyclist ahead?

Stay well back until there is an opportunity to overtake safely.

You should always be aware of the vulnerability of cyclists and other road users.

Give cyclists extra space, especially when are overtaking them – as they may swerve, wobble or change direction.

When stopped at traffic lights and the green light comes on but pedestrians are still crossing the road, what should a driver do?

Wait as long as necessary to enable them to complete the crossing.

A green traffic light means you should go if the way is clear. If pedestrians are crossing, give way to them and let them finish crossing before proceeding.

What should a driver do when they see a slow-moving vehicle ahead being driven by a learner driver?

Be patient and allow extra time to the driver if necessary.

Stay back until the slower vehicle can be overtaken safely.

You should be patient when driving behind a learner driver. Learners are not as experienced as other road users and may drive erratically.

What way is an inexperienced learner driver likely to react in traffic situations?

Slower then an experienced driver.

You should be patient when driving behind a learner driver. Learners may not anticipate and react to situations as well as an experienced driver would.

A driver sees a cyclist just ahead who is about to overtake a parked vehicle. There is no oncoming traffic, what should the driver do?

Allow the cyclist to overtake the parked vehicle and then proceed.

You should always read the road ahead and be prepared to react to changing traffic situations – in this case you should allow the cyclist ahead to overtake the parked car first.

In slow-moving traffic in a built-up area, what should a driver do when approaching a pedestrian crossing?

Time their stop/start movements to avoid obstructing the pedestrian crossing.

When you are in slow moving traffic and approaching a pedestrian crossing, you should not proceed onto the crossing unless you can clear it completely without stopping. Blocking a crossing could inconvenience pedestrians wishing to cross at that point.

At road junctions, what type of road users are particularly vulnerable?

Motorcyclists.
Pedestrians.
Cyclists.

Vehicles do not have an automatic right of way at junctions. As a driver you should pay particular attention to vulnerable road users such as pedestrians, cyclists and motorcyclists and be aware that they are entitled to use the road in safety.

At traffic lights, a driver should take particular care for which road users coming up on the left?

Cyclists.
Motorcyclists.

Before moving off at traffic lights you should be aware of cyclists and motorcyclists coming up on the left – in particular where there is an advanced stop line for cyclists ahead of that for other road users.

When a driver intends to make a left-hand turn on a busy city street junction and there are pedestrians and cyclists around, what should the driver do?

Watch for cyclists or pedestrians who may try to cross the road in front of the vehicle.

Watch for cyclists or pedestrians on the left.

Allow comfort space for any pedestrian on the left.

The vehicle does not have a greater right-of-way than any other road user.

As a driver you should pay particular attention to vulnerable road users such as pedestrians, cyclists and motorcyclists and be aware that they are entitled to use the road in safety.

In slow-moving city traffic, a driver should occasionally check their blind spots for which road users in particular?

Cyclists.
Motorcyclists.
Pedestrians.

In slow-moving city traffic, you should be aware of and check your blind spots before any manoeuvre. Pedestrians can easily become 'hidden' in a blind spot, and in slow-moving traffic, they might be moving faster than you are.

What should a driver do when approaching a junction with green traffic lights where there are elderly people crossing?

Allow them to cross in their own time.

When approaching a junction with green traffic lights, you should never assume that you have an automatic right of way. You should be aware that some road users (such as elderly pedestrians) may need extra time to clear the junction.

What should a driver do if the traffic light changes to green while pedestrians are still crossing at traffic lights or at a pelican crossing?

If the traffic lights change while pedestrians are still crossing at pelican crossings or traffic lights, what should a driver do?

Wait patiently and let them cross at ease.

You must always yield to pedestrians already crossing at a pedestrian crossing or junction, and you must not hurry them off the crossing by aggressive actions. Vehicles do not have a greater right of way over other road users.

What should a driver do if they see an elderly person crossing the road up ahead?

Reduce speed and let the person to complete the crossing safely.

You must not put pedestrians at risk, and you must give way to them while they are crossing. Be cautious and patient with pedestrians, particularly if they are elderly or infirm.

What should a driver do if while driving at 80km/h they see children on the road ahead?

Reduce speed and prepare to stop if necessary.

You should be aware that children can be unpredictable, and you should slow down and be prepared to stop if necessary.

Clearance

While you are driving, you should make sure that you leave room (clearance) for other road users, particularly the more vulnerable ones, such as pedestrians (especially children and elderly people), cyclists and motorcyclists.

What should a driver do when they see children just ahead on the road?

Give them a wide clearance and be prepared to slow down if necessary.

You should be aware that children can be unpredictable, and you should be prepared to slow down and give extra clearance to them if necessary.

When driving on a windy day and a cyclist is up ahead, what should a driver do?

Allow extra clearance in case the cyclist is blown off course.

You should never cut in front of cyclists when overtaking them. Give cyclists plenty of space especially in windy weather as they can easily be blown off course.

What should a driver do when overtaking a cyclist?

Allow extra clearance in case the cyclist swerves suddenly.

You should never cut in front of cyclists when overtaking them. Give them plenty of space especially as they may change direction suddenly – for example, to avoid a pothole, or because they are blown off course by a strong gust of wind.

What should a driver do when they see joggers ahead on the left?

Check the mirrors, indicate and overtake the joggers, allowing them sufficient clearance.

People on the road are more vulnerable than vehicles so you should treat them with care. If you see people jogging ahead, use the Mirror–Signal–Mirror (blind spots)–Manouevre routine and give sufficient clearance to the joggers when you are overtaking them.

When driving on a road that has a potholed surface and there is a cyclist ahead, what should a driver do?

Allow extra clearance in case the cyclist swerves to avoid a pothole.

You should always be aware of how vulnerable cyclists are. When you are driving on a road with potholes or bad surfaces, take into account that they may have to swerve suddenly to avoid potholes.

Anticipation

It is sometimes hard to predict what another road user is going to do, and some categories of road user are particularly unpredictable. You should be prepared for pedestrians crossing the road unexpectedly, for children chasing a ball, for dogs or other animals running onto the roadway, for cyclists swerving to avoid a pothole, and for people in parked cars opening the door without warning. The questions in this section check that you understand the importance of anticipating such events and that you know how to take appropriate action.

What precautions should a driver take in relation to pedestrians when driving in slow-moving traffic?

Watch for pedestrians who may cross the road in front of the vehicle.

In slow-moving city traffic, you should be aware of and check your blind spots before any manoeuvre. Pedestrians can easily become 'hidden' in a blind spot, and in slow-moving traffic, they might be moving faster than you are.

What should a driver be aware of when making a left-hand turn?

Check for pedestrians or cyclists who may have come up on the inside.

When you are turning left, you should be aware that cyclists and pedestrians may come up on your inside. Always check to your left before you make a left turn.

When driving through a residential area, what particular hazards should a driver be aware of?

Vehicles may drive or reverse onto the road.

Children or residents may come out suddenly.

When driving through a built-up area, you should drive with care and always be ready for the unexpected – such as other vehicles driving or reversing out onto the road unexpectedly or children running out onto the road.

When driving on a country road without footpaths, what should a driver look out for coming towards them on their side of the road?

Pedestrians.

Pedestrian deaths account for one in five fatalities on our roads, so you should always be on the look-out for pedestrians, especially on country roads where there is no footpath.

What should a driver do when driving at night on an unlit road?

Watch out for pedestrians wearing dark clothing.

Watch out for cars parked on the left.

Watch out for stray animals or livestock.

While driving at night and even with the best headlights, it can be very difficult to see all the hazards that you might come across – for example, stray animals or livestock on the road. At night you should drive at a speed that will enable you to stop safely within the distance you can see to be clear ahead.

What could happen if a driver parks on a footpath?

Pedestrians could be impeded.

You should never park on a footpath. Pedestrians (including people with young children in pushchairs and prams) might have to go onto the road to get around your car, and this could put them in danger.

Signalling

If you drive in such a way that other road users have to brake suddenly or change their course dramatically, you can cause a collision. For that reason, it is important to give other road users adequate warning of your intention to slow down, stop, or change direction. Use your indicators.

What should a driver do when driving along and there is a cyclist on the road up ahead?

Check the mirrors, indicate in good time and move out if it is safe to do so.

You should overtake only when it is safe to do so. Give extra space to cyclists when you are overtaking them, as they may need to move out to avoid a pothole, or they could be blown into your path on windy days.

If indicators are not fitted or are not working, how should signals be given?

By hand, clearly and in good time.

If, for whatever reason, your vehicle does not have indicators or has indicators that are not working, you should know how to use the appropriate hand signals to alert other road users of your intention to change direction.

What should a driver do when travelling on a country road with following traffic, and they meet pedestrians?

Signal to following traffic their intention to overtake the pedestrians.

When you are driving on a road without footpaths, you should take extra care when you come upon pedestrians on the road.

If you have to move out to overtake and there is following traffic, check your mirrors and signal in good time to alert the drivers behind that there is a hazard ahead.

Driving when the lighting is poor

At night, around dawn and dusk, and in bad weather, visibility can be significantly reduced. You need to keep a sharp look-out for other road users – particularly those that are more vulnerable, such as pedestrians and cyclists.

In relation to cyclists and pedestrians, what should a driver be aware of when driving on dark winter mornings and evenings on unlit country roads?

Cyclists and pedestrians are much more vulnerable in poor lighting conditions.

A driver should take extra care for cyclists and pedestrians in the countryside as they may not be clearly visible.

In relation to pedestrians, what should a driver be aware of when driving on dark winter mornings and evenings?

That there could be vulnerable pedestrians walking in the countryside.

Schoolchildren are more vulnerable on unlit country roads on dark winter mornings and evenings.

You should take extra care when driving on dark winter mornings and evenings – vulnerable road users such as cyclists and pedestrians (particularly schoolchildren) might not be so easy to see in low light conditions.

Necessary Documents

Before you drive any vehicle, you must hold a valid driving licence or learner permit for that category of vehicle, the vehicle must be properly taxed and insured, and you must be insured to drive it. You must carry your driving licence or learner permit with you while driving, and you must display up-to-date tax and insurance discs on the front windscreen of the vehicle.

Driving licences and learner permits

Your learner permit or driving licence imposes some restrictions on what you may and may not do when driving. The questions in this section check that you know the rules.

What drivers are required to display L-plates on their vehicle?

All learner permit holders except those driving agricultural tractors and works vehicles.

All learner permit holders except those driving agricultural tractors or works vehicles are required to display L-plates on the front and rear of their vehicle. Learner permit holders in category A1, A and M are required to wear a yellow fluorescent tabard with an L-plate that is clearly visible on the front and back.

What restriction will be noted on a driver's full licence if they have passed their test on a vehicle with automatic transmission?

They may not drive vehicles with manual transmission.

If you pass your driving test in a vehicle fitted with automatic transmission, a code 78 will be noted on the full licence in the restrictions / information column.

What roads are learner permit holders allowed to drive on?

All roads except motorways.

Which roads are learner permit holders not allowed to drive on?

They may not drive on motorways.

A learner permit holder must not drive on a motorway. It is a serious offence to do so.

How should an L-plate be composed?

A red L on a white background.

L-plates should be displayed front and rear. The plates should be a red L on a white background and should be not less than 15cm high with a border of at least 2cm.

A learner motorcyclist must wear a yellow tabard displaying L-plates front and rear. The L-plates must be not less than 15cm high on a white background.

Which learner permit holders are exempt from having to be accompanied by qualified drivers?

Learner permit holders in categories A, A1 and M.

Learner permit holders in categories A, A1 and M do not have to be accompanied by qualified drivers. Learner permit holders in these categories must not carry a passenger.

Where can drivers locate the Gross Vehicle Weight of their vehicle?

On a metal plate on the vehicle.

The plate displaying the Gross Vehicle Weight of a vehicle is normally located under the bonnet or in the passenger compartment. If you are not sure where it is located on your vehicle, check the driver's handbook supplied with the vehicle.

Vehicle registration and motor tax

Vehicles are registered when they are first sold or imported. The registration details are recorded in the vehicle registration document or vehicle licensing certificate – these details include the engine number and the vehicle registration number (which is shown on the registration plate at the front and back of the vehicle).

Vehicles that are used on public roads must be taxed at all times, and they must display a current tax disc at all times.

Is it permitted to use a vehicle in a public place without a current tax disc displayed?

No, all motor vehicles must be taxed before the vehicle is taken on the road.

If a driver wishes to drive a vehicle but the tax disc is expired, what should they do?

They should not drive it.

A motor vehicle must be taxed and must display the up-to-date tax disc before it may be taken on the road.

If a driver wishes to drive another vehicle which is not currently taxed, would they be allowed to transfer the current tax disc from their own vehicle onto it?

No, tax discs are not transferable.

A motor vehicle must be taxed and must display its own up-to-date tax disc before it may be taken on the road.

The tax disc includes information about the vehicle, including its make and model, colour and registration number.

When a vehicle is being driven by a person who is not its owner, who should ensure that the correct tax disc is displayed?

The driver and the owner of the vehicle are equally responsible.

A motor vehicle must be taxed before it may be taken on the road, and it must always display an up-to-date tax disc.

When must a current tax disc be displayed on a new vehicle on a public road?

At all times.

A motor vehicle must be taxed before it may be taken on the road, and it must always display an up-to-date tax disc.

Who may demand to see a driver's vehicle registration document or vehicle licensing certificate?

Any garda.

A garda may demand to see your driving licence at any time, and you should always carry this with you when driving. A garda may also examine your insurance disc, tax disc and NCT disc (if applicable). A garda may ask you to produce other documents (including the vehicle's registration document) at a named garda station within 10 days.

Insurance

Before you drive any vehicle, you must make sure that the vehicle is insured and that you are insured to drive it. It is a serious offence to drive without proper insurance. The questions in this section check that you fully understand this issue.

When a vehicle is being driven by a person who is not its owner but who has the owner's consent, who should ensure that the vehicle is properly insured?

Both the driver and the vehicle owner.

All drivers must have insurance covering them to drive a vehicle on a public road. It is a serious offence to drive a vehicle that is not insured. It is also an offence to allow a vehicle that you own to be driven by an uninsured driver.

Is a driver still insured to drive their vehicle after their insurance policy has expired?

No, the vehicle is not insured after the expiry of the policy.

All drivers must have insurance covering them to drive a vehicle on a public road. The vehicle must display an up-to-date insurance disc. Insurance companies insist that the premium must be paid before the renewal date.

If a driver wishes to drive another privately-owned vehicle but they are uncertain if they are insured to drive, what should they do?

A driver should contact their own insurer to confirm whether or not their insurance policy covers the driving of other vehicles.

When a driver wishes to drive a vehicle and they are not sure if they are covered by insurance, what should they do?

They should not drive until cover is confirmed by their insurance company.

If you are in any doubt about your insurance cover, you should discuss the matter with your insurance company. It is a serious offence to drive a vehicle that is not insured.

What is the minimum insurance cover which is required to drive a vehicle on a public road?

Third Party.

As a motorist, you must have a minimum of third party insurance. This indemnifies you against any claim made against you.

What information must a driver give in order to obtain insurance cover on a vehicle?

All information requested by the insurance company.

All drivers must have insurance covering them to drive a vehicle on a public road. The law imposes a duty on drivers to give their insurance company any relevant information before driving a vehicle.

If the owner of a vehicle has had the engine capacity of the vehicle altered, what should they do?

Inform their local motor taxation office and their insurance company.

The law imposes a duty on drivers to give their insurance company any relevant information before driving a vehicle. This includes details of any modifications made to the vehicle. In the case of a change of engine capacity, you must also inform the local Motor Taxation Office, as different rates of motor tax may apply.

What insurance details must be displayed on a vehicle's windscreen at all times?

The insurance disc.

It is an offence not to display an up-to-date insurance disc on your vehicle. Exceptions to this rule include tractors, vehicles showing a trade licence and some emergency services vehicles.

If a driver passes their test using a vehicle with automatic transmission, which vehicles are they licensed to drive?

Automatic vehicles only.

If you pass your driving test in an automatic or adapted vehicle, your full licence will apply to that type of vehicle only. A licence restricted to automatic vehicles will have a code 78 indicated in the restrictions / information column of the licence.

Collisions

At the scene of a collision, whether or not you were involved in it, your first concern should be to make sure that any injured persons are properly attended to by contacting the emergency services. Your second concern should be to make sure that the situation does not get any worse – this means making sure that oncoming traffic is given adequate warning of the hazard and that bystanders are not exposed to danger.

If the vehicle you are driving is involved in a collision, you must exchange information with the other driver, and you should report the incident to the Gardaí and to your insurance company.

Taking action

If you are involved in a collision, or if you arrive at the scene of a collision, you can help by calling the emergency services and by making sure that the situation does not get any worse. Do not take any action that might endanger yourself or anyone else, and administer first-aid only if you have been trained to do so.

How can a driver assist a motorcyclist who is in shock on the road following an incident?

Lie the motorcyclist on their side in the recovery position.

If you arrive at the scene of a collision, always call the emergency services on 999 or 112. Only properly trained persons should assist victims at the scene of an incident.

If a victim is conscious, you may help put them in the recovery position until the emergency services arrive. Never move a collision victim unless there is a danger of fire or of a vehicle turning over.

What should a driver do when involved in an incident where nobody is injured but the vehicles are causing a danger or obstruction on the road?

Mark the position of the vehicles and move them off the road.

In a collision where nobody is injured and there is only minor damage to vehicles, the vehicles should be moved to the side of the road to ensure that they do not cause an obstruction or endanger other road users.

What should a driver do if involved in an incident where they feel it was the fault of another driver?

Stop immediately and exchange particulars with the other person involved.

If you are involved in any sort of incident with another motorist, you should always exchange insurance details with the other driver and take note of the other vehicle's make and model, colour and registration number. You should report the incident to the Gardaí.

If a driver is involved in a collision, when should they inform their insurance company?

As soon as they possibly can.

If you are involved in an incident with another vehicle, you should inform your insurance company as soon as possible. This will help with any claims that may be made by another party against your insurance company.

Collision – no injury

If you are involved in a collision in which nobody is injured and the damage to property is minor, you do not have to involve the Gardaí. You should, however, exchange your contact details and insurance information with the other driver, and make a note of when, where and how the collision happened, in case the incident becomes the subject of an insurance claim later.

What must a driver do when involved in a collision where there is minor damage done to the vehicles?

Stop their vehicle and exchange particulars with the driver of the other vehicle.

If you are involved in a collision you must exchange details with the other driver, no matter how minor the damage is. What may look like minor damage at the time may turn out to be more serious when the vehicles are being repaired.

What should a driver do if involved in an incident where there is damage to property only?

It is not necessary to report it to the Gardaí provided it has been reported to the property owner.

If you are involved in an incident where the only damage is to property (for example, a garden wall or fence or a parked car), you must report it to the owner or to the person in charge of the property, or to the Gardaí if nearby. If you cannot do his, you should report the incident to a Garda station as soon as possible.

Collision – person injured

If you are involved in a collision and somebody is injured you must immediately contact the emergency services by dialling 112 or 999. You must stay at the scene of the collision and make a report to the Gardaí. You should if possible exchange your contact details and insurance information with the other driver. It is advisable to make a note of when, where and how the collision happened, so that you can provide these details to your insurance company.

What should a driver do where a person has been injured in a collision?

Move the victim only if there is a risk of fire or further injury.

Never move an injured person at the scene of a collision unless there is a risk of fire or further injury. Moving an injured person could add to their injuries. Trained personnel know best how to attend to injured persons.

Call the emergency services (on 999 or 112) or make sure that someone else has called them.

What type of drink should be given to a person who has been injured in a collision?

No drink should be given.

A person who has been injured in a collision should not be given anything to drink, as this could cause them to choke. Only trained personnel should attend to an injured person. Call the emergency services (on 999 or 112) or make sure that someone else has called them.

What should a driver do to assist a person who is unconscious following a collision?

Loosen tight clothing around the neck and keep the person warm with a blanket or overcoat.

If a person is unconscious following a collision, you should loosen tight clothing around the their neck and keep them warm with a blanket or overcoat until the emergency services arrive.

Call the emergency services (on 999 or 112) or make sure that someone else has called them.

What should a driver do if they arrive at the scene of a collision and a person is bleeding heavily?

Try to stop the bleeding by putting on a tight bandage.

If you arrive at the scene of a collision and someone is bleeding heavily, you can try to stop the flow of blood by putting on a tight bandage.

Call the emergency services (on 999 or 112) or make sure that someone else has called them.

What is the correct procedure where somebody has been injured in a collision?

Do not move the person unless there is a danger of fire or of being hit by passing vehicles.

Never move an injured person at the scene of a collision unless there is a risk of fire or further injury. Moving an injured person could make their injuries worse.

Call the emergency services (on 999 or 112) or make sure that someone else has called them.

Who should first be contacted where a person has been injured in a collision?

Who should be contacted where a driver is involved in a collision where a person is injured?

The emergency services.

If you are involved in a collision where someone has been injured, contact the emergency services immediately on 999 or 112. Trained emergency services personnel know best how to attend to injured persons.

Exchange of information

If you are involved in a collision with another vehicle, you should ask the driver of the other vehicle for their contact details (name, address, telephone number) and the details of their insurance cover (insurance company and policy number). You should also note the registration number, make and model of their vehicle. At the same time, you should provide the other driver with your own details and those of your vehicle. You will need all these details to report the incident to the Gardaí or to your insurance company.

If a driver is involved in a collision with an uninsured visiting motorist, where nobody is injured, who should it be reported to?

The driver's insurance company and the Gardaí.

If you are involved in any type of collision, you should always report it to the Gardaí and to your insurance company.

What should a driver do if involved in a collision with another vehicle where nobody is injured?

Exchange all relevant details with the other driver and report it to the Gardaí.

If a you are involved in a collision with another vehicle where nobody is injured, you should exchange all the relevant details with the other driver – including name, address, vehicle registration, make and model and all insurance details.

Hazardous materials

If you are involved in a collision with a vehicle carrying hazardous materials, or if you arrive at the scene of such a collision, you should take steps to make sure that the situation does not deteriorate. Do not take any action that might endanger yourself or others. Call the emergency services and try to warn other road users of the danger.

What should a driver do if they arrive at the scene of a collision involving a vehicle carrying hazardous materials?

Keep well clear and raise the alarm.

If you arrive at the scene of a collision involving a vehicle carrying hazardous materials, you should keep well clear of the scene. Call the emergency services on 999 or 112 and give them as much information as you can about the marking labels on the vehicle. You should also warn other road users about the danger.

Safety considerations relating to loads and passengers

The questions in this section are designed to check that you understand the effects of severe braking on the people and goods in your vehicle, and that you know the importance of keeping the loads you carry in the vehicle within the limits set by the manufacturer.

Severe braking

By planning your journey, reading the road ahead, developing an awareness of the traffic conditions around you, and driving at an appropriate speed, you can generally avoid the need for sudden or harsh braking. On the occasions when you do have to apply the brakes severely, you need to be aware of the effects on yourself, your passengers and any goods in the vehicle.

What danger can arise if a driver has to brake suddenly?

Both the driver and passengers could be thrown forward.

When you brake suddenly, the balance of weight of the vehicle is shifted forward, and this may cause the occupants and any loose objects in the vehicle to be thrown forward.

What should a driver do to avoid the need for harsh braking?

Look ahead and anticipate what others may do.

You should know what speed you're travelling at, you should always drive at a speed that is appropriate to the conditions you are driving in, and you should be able to stop smoothly and safely within the distance you can see to be clear ahead.

Vehicle carrying capacity and load distribution

Every vehicle is certified by its manufacturer to have a maximum safe load-carrying capacity, and a maximum towing capacity. You must not exceed these limits: it is illegal to do so, and can be extremely dangerous. The questions in this section check that you understand this important issue.

How does the driver know a vehicle's total load-carrying capacity?

By referring to the vehicle manufacturer's specification.

Design Gross Vehicle Weight is the term used by manufacturers for the weight of the vehicle together with the maximum load it is designed to carry. Drivers must understand the carrying capacity of their vehicle. Overloading your vehicle will make it more difficult to control, and it's an offence.

What determines the maximum allowed towing capacity of a vehicle?

The manufacturer's specifications.

The maximum weight that your vehicle can safely tow is specified by the manufacturer, and is usually set out in the driver's handbook for the vehicle, and in some cases on a plate attached to the vehicle.

This is the safe towing limit for the vehicle and you should not exceed it.

What effect does overloading a vehicle have on its road-holding?

The load can make the vehicle more difficult to control.

Overloading your vehicle will make it more difficult to control.

Remember: it's an offence to overload a vehicle.

What would be the effect of overloading a vehicle with passengers or goods?

It would reduce the driver's ability to control the vehicle.

Overloading your vehicle will make it more difficult to control, and will increase the risk of a collision.

What effect could an unevenly distributed load have on a vehicle?

It could make the vehicle unstable while turning a corner or braking.

When loading a vehicle you should ensure that the load is distributed evenly. An unevenly distributed load may change the vehicle's centre of gravity and this could affect the braking and steering.

Technical matters with a bearing on road safety

The questions in this section check that you know how to keep your vehicle in good condition, that you recognise signs that it needs to be repaired or serviced, and that you understand the implications for your own safety and that of others of a vehicle in poor condition.

Headlights

When you are driving at night or in poor visibility, the headlights on your vehicle are essential for two reasons: they enable you to see the road ahead, and they enable other drivers and road users to see your vehicle. For these reasons, the headlights on the vehicle must be working properly at all times.

Why is it important to ensure that the vehicle headlights are correctly aligned?

To enable the driver to see properly.

You should ensure that your headlights are properly aligned and clean. When dipped, properly aligned headlights are less likely to dazzle oncoming traffic.

Which part of the car must be maintained in good condition?

Headlights.
Seatbelts.

You are responsible for your vehicle's roadworthiness and you should check it at regular intervals. Among the checks you should make are that all the lights (including the headlights) and all the seatbelts (driver's and passengers') are in good working order.

What is the effect of incorrectly aimed headlights?

The headlights will not shine light correctly on the road ahead.

What effect could incorrectly aligned headlights have?

They could dazzle oncoming drivers.

Incorrectly aimed (or aligned) headlights can dazzle oncoming traffic, even when dipped, and they are not as effective at lighting the road ahead. For these reasons, you should ensure that your vehicle's headlights are clean and properly aligned.

In general, how frequently should a vehicle's lights be checked?

Regularly.

What effect can a broken lens have on a headlight?

It can reduce and distort the beam.

You are responsible for your vehicle's roadworthiness and you should check it at regular intervals. Among the checks you should make are that all the lights are in working order. If you find defects in the lights, you should have them repaired as soon as possible.

A driver wishes to drive at night, but their right-hand headlight bulb is blown. What should the driver do?

Not drive until the bulb is replaced.

You must not drive on the road unless your vehicle's headlights are in good working order and adjusted properly.

Brake lights

The brake lights on your vehicle provide a visible warning to traffic coming behind you that you are slowing and may be stopping. They must be kept in working order.

How would a driver know if a brake-light bulb was not working?

By standing at the rear of the vehicle and checking as another person presses the brake pedal.

To help you to be sure that the rear brake lights are working correctly, ask someone to stand outside the car and to check that the lights come on when you press the brake pedal.

Is it permissible to drive a vehicle on a public road when the brake lights are not working?

No, it is never permitted to be driven.

You must ensure that your vehicle's brake-lights are clean and working correctly before driving on a public road.

Dashboard lights

Modern engines are equipped with sophisticated systems for monitoring the condition of the engine and other parts of the vehicle, and for warning the driver if something goes wrong. These warnings are generally in the form of a warning light on the dashboard.

What does this light mean?

The battery is not charging.

If the battery warning light comes on, it means there is some kind of problem with the electrical charging system of the vehicle and the battery isn't being charged properly.

What does this light mean?

The high-beam headlights are switched on.

All vehicles are fitted with warning lights to alert you to different things. This light comes on when your full beam headlights are turned on.

What does this light mean?

Low oil level.

If the oil pressure warning light comes on, it means that the oil pressure has dropped. You should not drive the vehicle until the problem is fixed.

What does this light mean?

Directional indicator on.

All vehicles are fitted with warning lights to alert you to different things. This light tells you that the directional indicator is on.

What should a driver do if a warning light starts flashing on the dashboard of their vehicle?

Stop and check the problem.

What should a driver do if a red warning light lights up on the dashboard of their vehicle?

Stop and investigate the cause.

If a warning light comes on while you are driving, you should stop in a safe place and investigate the problem before deciding what action to take.

Reflectors

What is the purpose of the vehicle's reflectors?

They reflect light at night to make other road users aware of the vehicle.

Motor vehicles are fitted with reflectors to make it easier to be seen by other road users. Keep your reflectors clean to ensure they are most effective.

Indicators

When a driver operates the indicator switch and hears a more rapid clicking noise than normal, what could this mean?

An indicator bulb has blown.

A rapid clicking noise when you turn on an indicator is usually a sign that one of the indicator bulbs has failed.

You are responsible for making sure that your vehicle is roadworthy. This should include a regular check that all your lights, including indicators, are working properly.

Brakes

You must keep the brakes in your vehicle in working order at all times, so that you can control the speed of the vehicle and stop it when and where you want to.

What does ABS do?

It prevents the wheels from locking under harsh braking conditions.

Anti-lock braking system (ABS) is a type of braking system found in most modern cars. It comes into play automatically when you brake harshly. In the wet it can help prevent the wheels from skidding so that you can continue to steer while braking. ABS does not reduce the braking distance.

If the brake pedal of a vehicle feels soft or spongy when applied, what does this mean?

A fault in the brake fluid system.

How would a driver know if the brake fluid in their vehicle is low?

The brakes feel spongy and soft.

If the brake pedal feels soft or spongy when you press it, it could indicate that the brake fluid level is low and there is a fault in the system.

Check the brake fluid level regularly, and test the brakes each time you set out on a journey.

What is a possible consequence of driving a vehicle in which the brake fluid level is low?

The vehicle could fail to stop when the brakes are applied, leading to a collision.

For your brakes to work correctly, you need to make sure that the brake fluid is kept at the correct level.

If the brake fluid is low, the brakes will feel spongy or soft, they won't work as well as they should and this will increase your stopping distance. Low brake fluid could be the difference between stopping safely and having a collision.

If a driver applies the foot brake and hears a scraping noise, what is the most likely cause?

The brake linings or pads are worn.

You should test your brakes before setting out on a journey. If while driving you hear a scraping noise when you press the brake, the most likely reason is that the brake linings or pads are worn.

In this case, your brakes won't work as well as they should. Have worn brake linings or pads replaced immediately.

How does a driver know when there is a problem with the brakes in their vehicle?

The vehicle's stopping ability is affected.

You should test your brakes before setting out on a journey. If when you are braking you notice that it takes longer than usual to bring the vehicle to a stop, you should have the brakes checked by a mechanic immediately.

Automatic transmission

A vehicle with automatic transmission has some obvious differences from one with manual transmission (such as no clutch), and some differences that are not so obvious. You need to be aware of these differences, particularly if you sometimes drive a manual vehicle and sometimes an automatic.

If driving a vehicle with automatic transmission, what in particular should a driver be aware of?

That engine braking power is reduced.

What effect does automatic transmission have on engine braking power?

It reduces it.

When you are driving an automatic vehicle and you release the accelerator, the vehicle will not slow at the same rate as a vehicle with a manual gearbox. You should be aware of this, as you may need to apply the brake earlier in order to stop where required.

Vehicle condition (engine)

For your comfort and safety, and those of your passengers and other road users, you should make sure that the engine in your vehicle is operating properly. Have it serviced regularly, in line with the manufacturer's recommendations.

What does this dial provide information on?

What does a rev counter provide information on?

Engine revolutions.

The rev counter measures the speed of the engine. in 'revolutions per minute' (RPM). Generally, the higher the revs, the more fuel the engine is using, so you should keep an eye on the rev counter to help you drive in a more eco-friendly manner.

If, when driving along, the driver notices that the engine power is lower than normal, what should they do?

Have the vehicle checked by a competent mechanic.

If when driving you notice that the vehicle seems underpowered, you should have it checked by a competent mechanic as soon as possible. This could be a symptom of one of a number of problems.

Oil and fuel

The oil in your engine lubricates and cools the moving parts of the engine. If there is too little oil in the engine, or if it is not reaching the parts that need it, the engine can be permanently damaged.

You should, of course, make sure that you have sufficient fuel (petrol or diesel, depending on the type of engine) in the tank to take you safely to your destination.

What is the purpose of engine oil?

It lubricates the engine components.

The purpose of engine oil is to lubricate and cool the moving parts of the engine.

If the oil gauge shows little or no pressure, what could the problem be?

The oil level is too low.

You should check the oil level in your vehicle regularly, and if it is low, top it up.

If you find you have to top up very often, you should have the vehicle checked by a mechanic to see if there is a problem.

What may happen if the vehicle's engine oil is not changed regularly?

Parts of the engine may suffer increased wear.

Engine oil becomes dirty over time and must be changed. The oil change is usually done when the vehicle is being serviced.

If a vehicle is driven with low oil pressure, what effect does this have on its engine?

It increases wear and tear on the engine.

Low oil pressure is usually related to low oil level or to a faulty oil pump. You should check the oil level in your vehicle regularly, and if it is low, top it up.

If you find you have to top up very often, you should have the vehicle checked by a mechanic to see if there is a problem.

If the vehicle's oil-pressure gauge is reading low or the red oil-pressure warning light comes on, what should a driver do?

Drive to a safe place, stop the vehicle and check the oil level.

Oil circulation is essential for the safe running of your vehicle's engine. If the warning lights or gauges tell you that the oil is low or the pressure is low, you should stop as soon as you can in safe place, check the oil level, and top up if necessary. Continuing to drive may damage the engine.

If the problem is not just related to the oil level, you should have the vehicle checked by a mechanic.

What should someone do before checking the engine oil level on a vehicle?

Make sure that the engine is switched off.

You should have a basic knowledge of the regular checks that should be carried out on your vehicle. Checking the engine oil level is important – do this with the engine switched off.

What is the function of an engine oil filter?

It prevents the circulation of sediment in the oil.

The oil filter collects impurities and sediment from the oil and so helps to reduce damage and wear and tear on the engine. The oil filter must be changed regularly – this is usually done when the vehicle is being serviced.

While driving, a driver notices a strong smell of fuel. What should they do?

Stop where safe and investigate.

A strong smell of fuel is usually an indication that something is wrong, and you should stop and investigate as soon as possible. Leaking or spilling petrol can be dangerous because it is so combustible, and leaking diesel fuel can make the road very slippery.

What does the warning light and/or red zone on a fuel gauge mean?

The level of fuel in the tank is low.

Many vehicles are fitted with various warning lights and gauges. A red zone or a warning light on a fuel gauge means the vehicle is low in fuel and should be refuelled as soon as possible.

Coolant temperature

While it is running, the engine in your vehicle heats up, but if it overheats, it may be permanently damaged. To prevent this, the main parts of the engine are kept at the correct temperature by the circulation of cooling fluid. You must make sure that there is sufficient coolant in the reservoir, and that you do not drive if the temperature gauge or warning light indicates that the engine is overheating.

When is it recommended to use coolant or antifreeze?

All year round.

The purpose of coolant is to keep the engine cool during operation. Coolant is usually a mixture of water and antifreeze – this ensures that the coolant does not freeze in very cold weather.

While driving, the driver notices the vehicle temperature gauge showing red. What should they do?

Stop in a safe place and have the problem investigated.

Many vehicles are fitted with various warning lights and gauges. A warning light or a red zone on a temperature gauge means the engine is starting to overheat and the vehicle should not be driven until the problem is rectified.

What should a driver do if they notice steam rising from the engine compartment?

Stop where safe and investigate the cause.

When a vehicle shows signs of overheating, you should stop in a safe place and investigate the problem. Do not drive a vehicle whose engine is overheating, as this could damage the engine.

Body condition

If the body of your vehicle is damaged or rusted, it can be more dangerous. For example, if there are sharp or jagged edges, these can cause serious injury if the vehicle is involved in a collision – even a minor one. You should also ensure that the shock absorbers are functioning correctly, or the vehicle may become unstable and difficult to control.

If a driver notices that parts of their vehicle's body have been affected by rust, what should they do?

Have it repaired by a competent repair shop.

Over time, vehicles may become affected by rust to various degrees. You should inspect your vehicle's body periodically and if you find signs of rust you should have it assessed and repaired if necessary to prevent further deterioration.

What effect can a worn shock absorber have on a vehicle?

It can cause the vehicle to 'bounce' in an unstable manner.

A worn shock absorber can make a vehicle difficulty to control especially on uneven surfaces and it can increase stopping distance.

Battery

In a petrol- or diesel-powered vehicle, the engine is started by a small electric motor, which is powered by a 12-volt battery. This battery also supplies power to the lights and other electrical appliances, but only when the engine is not running. When the engine is running, it drives an alternator to produce electricity, and this both recharges the battery and supplies power to the lights and other electrical appliances.

What happens if the vehicle has a flat battery?

The engine will not start.

All motor vehicles have a battery to supply power, primarily to start the engine. If the battery is flat, you will not be able to start the engine in the normal way.

When the engine is running, it produces its own electricity to recharge the battery and run the various electrical components, including lights, heating, the radio and so on.

What is the purpose of the battery fitted to a petrol- or diesel-powered motor vehicle?

To start the engine.

The primary purpose of the battery is to start the engine.

When the engine is running, it produces its own electricity to charge the battery and run the various electrical components, including lights, heating, radio and so on.

What effect would a weakly charged battery have on a vehicle's driving performance?

It would have no effect.

It might be difficult to start a car with a weak battery, but once the engine is running, it makes no difference.

You should replace the battery before it runs out completely.

Mirrors

The exterior mirrors on each side of the vehicle and the interior rear-view mirror are important pieces of safety equipment. While you are driving, they enable you to see behind and to the side of your vehicle without turning your head, so that you can maintain your view of the road ahead. Before starting a journey, you should make sure that they are in good condition and properly adjusted.

What should the driver be able to see in the vehicle mirrors when they have been properly adjusted?

The area behind and to each side of the vehicle.

Your mirrors enable you to see the road behind and to the sides. This helps you to take into account what's happening behind you, so that you can make informed, correct and safe decisions.

What should the driver be able to see in the exterior mirrors of a vehicle when they have been properly adjusted?

The sides of the vehicle and the roads to the side.

Exterior mirrors enable you to see to the side of the vehicle, and to take into account all visible hazards and make correct and safe decisions.

The vehicle's exterior mirrors are covered by a film of mud and dust. What should the driver do?

Clean them with a cloth or tissue before continuing on.

Keep your mirrors clean and properly adjusted, so that your view of the road to the rear and the sides is clear and unhindered.

When a driver is making a left-hand turn, what mirrors should they particularly concentrate on?

The interior and left exterior mirror.

When you are turning left, you should be aware that cyclists and other vehicles may come up on your inside. For that reason it is particularly important to check your left exterior mirror and your internal mirror before turning.

Always use the Mirror–Signal–Mirror (blind spots)–Manouevre routine when you are turning and be extra careful If you have to cross a bus lane to make the turn.

What effect can wet weather have on a vehicle's exterior mirrors?

Water droplets can obscure the reflected image.

In rain and damp conditions, small water droplets can form on the glass of the exterior mirrors. This could make it more difficult to see the road behind and to the sides.

Switch on the mirror demisters, if you have them.

Exhaust

The exhaust system on a vehicle takes away the gases and other by-products of the engine's combustion process. In doing so, it filters them to make them less damaging to the environment, and it reduces the noise created by the engine. It is important to make sure that the exhaust system is in good condition – if it is not working correctly, poisonous fumes may enter the vehicle, with lethal consequences.

What does blue smoke coming from the vehicle's exhaust mean?

The engine is burning oil.

As an engine gets old or if it is not properly maintained, it can 'burn oil' and give off 'blue smoke' from the exhaust. This is harmful to the atmosphere and should be corrected.

What is the effect of a worn exhaust?

The filtering of fumes is reduced and engine noise is louder.

How can a faulty exhaust affect your vehicle?

It can increase the noise and pollution levels.

A worn or faulty exhaust system can have a number of effects, including increased noise from the engine and more fumes (as they are not filtered properly).

What is the purpose of a catalytic converter?

It filters exhaust gases and reduces air pollution.

The purpose of a catalytic converter (CAT) is to remove toxic or polluting gases such as carbon monoxide, nitrogen oxide and unburned hydrocarbons from the exhaust emissions.

Tyres and wheels

Your ability to control your vehicle, to steer it in the direction you want and to stop it when and where you want depends critically on the few square centimetres of rubber that are in contact with the road at any time. You must make sure that your tyres are in good condition and correctly inflated. The questions in this section check that you know how to do this.

What does the speed rating of a tyre indicate?

The maximum speed for which the tyre is designed.

The speed rating of a tyre is the maximum speed for which the tyre is designed. This relates to the speed capability of the tyre. It does not relate to the speed at which the tyre should or could legally be driven.

Why should the valve be replaced when having a tubeless tyre fitted?

To ensure the tyre will stay inflated.

When fitting a new tubeless tyre to a vehicle it is a good idea to change the valve also, because it has presumably been on the wheel since the old tyre was fitted; and it could break down, leak and cause the air to escape.

After changing a wheel on a vehicle, what should be checked soon afterwards?

The wheel nuts.

The tyre pressure.

A short period after you have changed a wheel on a vehicle, you should check

- The tyre pressure, to make sure it is correct; and
- The wheel nuts, to ensure they are still properly secured.

In general, how often should a driver check the tyre pressure of a vehicle?

Regularly.

As a driver, it is your legal responsibility to make sure that your vehicle is roadworthy. To do this, you should carry out weekly and periodical checks, including a weekly tyre pressure check.

Why should tyres be kept at the pressure specified by the manufacturer?

To help provide optimum roadholding.

The vehicle manufacturer specifies the pressure to which tyres on a vehicle should be inflated. This is the pressure that gives the best performance in road holding, efficient braking and fuel consumption.

Most manufacturers specify different pressures for front and rear tyres.

A fault in what component would lead to uneven or excessive tyre wear?

Suspension.

If a vehicle has a worn suspension it may lead to uneven or excessive tyre wear. If you notice that your tyres are unevenly worn, you should investigate the reason and have it repaired.

What effect would under-inflated tyres have on a vehicle's transmission?

It would have no effect on it.

Incorrect tyre pressure does not affect the engine transmission.

What can be affected by driving on under-inflated tyres?

Fuel consumption.

Braking ability.

What is the effect of under-inflated tyres on a vehicle?

Impaired braking and steering.

What can be adversely affected by under-inflated tyres?

Steering.

What effect does low tyre-pressure have on a vehicle?

Braking and cornering are impaired.

Under-inflated tyres can increase the effort required to steer the vehicle. Always make sure the tyres are properly inflated by checking the tyre pressures regularly.

Incorrect tyre pressure adversely affects many of a vehicle's systems, including brakes, suspension, steering and fuel consumption.

When should tyre pressure be checked?

When the tyres are cold.

You should check the tyre pressure in your vehicle once a week. Do this when the tyres are cold, using a reliable gauge.

Tyres should always be inflated according to the vehicle manufacturer's guidelines.

During a weekly check, a driver notices a badly worn front tyre. What should they do?

Have the worn tyre replaced.

The quality of the tyres on a vehicle is an important factor in the vehicle's road holding and braking ability.

So if you notice that a tyre is badly worn, you should replace it as soon as possible. The minimum legal tread depth for tyres on most vehicles is 1.6mm, but you should replace a tyre before it becomes this worn.

What effect could hitting or mounting the kerb have on a vehicle's tyres?

It could damage the sidewalls.

If a vehicle hits or mounts the kerb it could damage the sidewall of the tyre. If that happens it could cause the tyre to 'blow-out' later. If it happens at high speed the vehicle could go out of control and crash.

What does worn tread along the edge of a tyre suggest?

Steering alignment may be faulty.

If you notice that a tyre on your vehicle is worn along its edge, this may indicate a problem with the steering alignment. This is a potentially dangerous problem, and you should have it fixed as soon as possible.

What should a driver do before undertaking a long journey?

Check the tyres are inflated to normal air pressure.

It is important to check the tyre pressure before starting a long journey as incorrect air pressure can adversely affect many of the vehicle's systems, including brakes, steering, suspension and fuel consumption.

Under what circumstances should a driver increase the air pressure in the tyres before undertaking a long journey?

Never.

Check the air pressure before you start a long journey, and when you inflate the tyres, make sure that you follow the vehicle manufacturer's recommended tyre pressure This is the pressure that gives the best performance in road holding, efficient braking and fuel consumption.

What should the driver do to secure the vehicle when changing a wheel?

Ensure that the vehicle cannot roll when jacked up.

If you have to change a wheel, make sure you do it in a safe place on level ground. Also, apply the handbrake and engage a low gear to secure the vehicle before you jack it up.

What effect would coasting have on a vehicle's tyres?

No effect.

Coasting is a bad practice that happens when a driver allows a vehicle to move by its own momentum (or by gravity – for example, down a hill) with the engine disengaged. This can be done in two ways:

1. By putting the car into neutral gear while moving; or
2. By keeping the clutch pedal pressed down to disengage the selected gear.

If a vehicle is coasting, the driver has much less control, so you should never coast. However, it has no effect on the tyres.

While driving, what does a continuous vibration in the steering indicate?

The wheel balance is uneven.

If you feel a continuous vibration in the steering, particularly at higher speeds, this could indicate that the balance of the vehicle wheels is uneven. If this is the case, you should have it investigated by a mechanic.

What can cause heavy steering?

Under-inflated tyres.

Heavy steering is when you need to use more effort than usual to turn the steering wheel. You might experience this if the power-assisted steering system is not working properly, or more commonly, if the front tyres are under-inflated.

Clutch

In vehicles with manual transmission, the clutch enables the driver to disengage the engine from the transmission. This allows the engine to continue running while the vehicle is stopped, and makes it easy for the driver to change gears. In a car, the clutch is generally operated by the left-most pedal; on a motorcycle it is operated by a lever on the left handlebar.

Between the extremes of fully engaged and fully disengaged, the clutch transmits a varying proportion of the engine's force to the transmission, but it becomes very hot, and if you over-use the clutch it can become damaged ('burnt out'). For this reason you should avoid driving for long periods with the clutch partially engaged.

When driving, where should a driver rest their left foot?

On the floor or foot rest.

The clutch is the connection between the engine and the gearbox. It enables the vehicle to move when a gear is engaged. You should not rest your foot on the clutch pedal because it may disengage the selected gear or damage the clutch mechanism.

Environmental matters

Motor vehicles are a significant cause of pollution. All drivers should be aware of this, and should modify their driving habits to minimise their negative impact on the environment.

Minimising environmental impact

The questions in this section check that you understand environmental issues about driving, and you know how to drive in an environmentally responsible manner.

In what way do motor vehicles harm the environment?

By increasing carbon monoxide levels.

Carbon monoxide is a poisonous gas emitted by vehicle exhausts into the atmosphere. Driving economically and keeping a vehicle well maintained can reduce the level of carbon monoxide emissions.

What can a driver do to help the environment?

Read the road and plan ahead.

Reduce speed.

Drivers should plan well ahead, drive smoothly and avoid harsh acceleration and braking. Vehicles travelling at 112km/h use up to 30% more fuel than those travelling at 80km/h. However, you should not drive so slow as to inconvenience other road users.

What alternatives can drivers take to help protect the environment?

Use public transport.

Using public transport helps to protect the environment. Buses, trams and trains are a more environmentally friendly way to move large numbers of people especially in urban areas. Consider using public transport where possible – not only is it more environmentally friendly, but it can also be more cost-effective when you take the cost of fuel and parking charges into account.

What can drivers do to help protect the environment?

Car share.

Car sharing helps the environment. Drivers should consider car sharing for routine journeys to work or for the school run. This will reduce pollution and reduce traffic congestion at peak times.

What can be achieved by the driving style known as 'eco-driving'?

Reduced fuel consumption.

Increased road safety.

Reduced emissions.

The advantages of 'eco-driving' include improved road safety, improved fuel consumption and reduced emissions. The eco-conscious driver becomes a more efficient driver because they learn to read the road further ahead and display better anticipation skills. This reduces the need for harsh acceleration and braking which results in a more economical style of driving and a smoother drive.

Which action contributes to eco-driving?

Selecting a high gear as soon as possible.

Maintaining a steady speed.

Looking ahead and anticipating.

'Eco driving' contributes to road safety and also reduces fuel consumption and harmful emissions. Eco-conscious drivers read the road well ahead and anticipate what is going to happen in front.

This reduces the need for harsh acceleration and braking which results in a more comfortable and safer drive while saving fuel and reducing emissions.

Fuel consumption

Driving in such a way that you minimise your consumption of fuel is good for you and it's good for the planet. It saves you money, it uses less of a scarce resource, and it produces less pollution. It is also safer. These questions check that you know how to maximise your fuel efficiency.

What can a driver do to maximise fuel efficiency while driving?

Avoid carrying unnecessary weight.

The more extra weight is in your vehicle, the more fuel you use.

Using a roof rack or a roof box increases wind resistance and this also increases fuel consumption – by as much as 15%. Remove roof racks and roof boxes when not in use.

Which action is likely to cause an increase in fuel consumption?

Harsh acceleration.

Harsh acceleration increases fuel consumption. Driving smoothly reduces wear and tear and also improves fuel consumption. Use the highest gear possible without causing the engine to labour.

What should a driver do to minimise fuel consumption in their vehicle?

Use gentle acceleration and braking.

Driving smoothly will help reduce your fuel consumption. Read the road ahead and adjust your speed in good time, and avoid harsh acceleration and late braking.

How does harsh acceleration affect fuel consumption?

Fuel consumption increases.

Harsh acceleration increases fuel consumption, and driving smoothly helps to reduce your fuel consumption and the emissions from your vehicle.

Try not to over-rev the engine and use the appropriate gear for the speed of the vehicle. When slowing down, take your foot off the accelerator and allow the vehicle to slow progressively before you brake.

How does continuous high-speed driving affect fuel consumption?

It increases fuel consumption.

Driving at high speeds increases your fuel consumption. A vehicle travelling at 112km/h uses approximately 30% more fuel than one travelling at 80km/h.

What should a driver do to ensure better fuel efficiency from their vehicle?

Ensure that the vehicle is regularly serviced.

One of the keys to good fuel efficiency is making sure that your vehicle is well maintained. Servicing should be carried out as recommended by the manufacturer.

Checking the tyre pressure regularly can also help ensure good fuel efficiency.

How can fuel efficiency be improved?

By using gentle acceleration and making gear changes appropriate to speed.

The way you drive can contribute to your vehicle's fuel efficiency:

- Accelerate gently;
- Use the highest available gear (without causing the engine to struggle); and
- Drive smoothly – this also reduces wear and tear on a vehicle.

Noise

Motor vehicles make a lot of noise. You should try to make sure that your vehicle and your style of driving do not create so much noise that they cause a nuisance to others.

What effect does a worn exhaust have on a vehicle?

It causes noise and gas pollution levels to increase.

A vehicle with a worn exhaust will probably be noisier and will produce more polluting emissions.

There are strict regulations governing the noise and emission levels of vehicles, and these are rigorously checked during a vehicle's NCT.

When is the use of the horn prohibited?

Between 11:30pm and 7:00am in a built-up area.

Is a driver allowed to sound the horn while driving in a built-up area at night?

Yes, but between 11:30pm and 7:00am the horn may be sounded only in an emergency.

You are not allowed to use the horn in a built-up area between 11:30pm and 7:00am unless there is a traffic emergency. Only use a horn to warn other road users of oncoming danger or if you need to make them aware of your presence for safety reasons. Using the horn does not give you an automatic right of way. Never use the horn to provoke a reaction from or to rebuke another motorist.

Under what circumstances is it permitted to replace the standard horn on a vehicle with a musical horn?

Never.

A horn is designed to be an audible warning device. You should not make any technical modifications to the horn without professional advice as these may have legal and safety implications.

Taking corrective or emergency action

When you are driving, you need to always expect the unexpected. You literally don't know what's around the next bend, but you can avoid some dangerous situations by developing your observation skills and learning to anticipate danger. Even the best and safest drivers, however, will have to take corrective or emergency actions from time to time.

Skidding

You should always drive in a way that is suited to the weather conditions and the state of the road. If you do, you will generally avoid skidding. However, if you do find yourself in a skid, you must know how to react in order to get the vehicle back into control as soon as possible. These questions check that you understand the causes of skidding and how to avoid them.

What can cause a vehicle to skid?

Using harsh acceleration.

Excessively heavy braking.

Excessive speed.

Using harsh acceleration at the wrong time can cause a vehicle to skid, especially if the road is wet.

Heavy braking can cause a vehicle to skid, particularly if the road surface is wet or uneven, or if the tyres are worn or incorrectly inflated. Read the road well ahead and try to avoid heavy braking, particularly in wet or slippery conditions.

Excessive speed can also result in a vehicle going into a skid. You should always drive at a safe speed and never exceed the speed limit for the road you are on. Excessive speed is particularly dangerous in wet and slippery conditions.

Punctures

A puncture is always an inconvenience, but it is also sometimes dangerous. If you get a sudden puncture while driving, you must know what to do in order to keep control of the vehicle and not endanger yourself or others.

What should a driver do if a front tyre bursts?

Grip the steering wheel firmly.

> If a front tyre bursts on a vehicle, the steering on the vehicle will become unstable.
>
> Don't panic – slow down gradually while keeping a firm hold on the steering wheel. Stop in a safe place to change the wheel, and alert other road users by switching on your hazard warning lights.

What should a driver do if their vehicle gets a puncture on a motorway?

Pull in where safe on the hard shoulder and call for assistance.

> Don't try to change a wheel on a motorway, as this could be very dangerous. Drive the car on to the hard shoulder, and when it is safe to do so, get out of the vehicle and move behind the barrier. Call for assistance from a motorway emergency phone or using a mobile phone (call the Gardaí).

Fire

Fire in a vehicle is rare, but if it does occur it can be very dangerous, both for the people in the vehicle and for others in the vicinity. You should know the precautions to take against fire, and know what to do if fire does break out in your vehicle.

What precautions could a driver take against the risk of fire in their vehicle?

Investigate strong fumes and carry a fire extinguisher.

> A strong smell of fuel is usually an indication that something is wrong, and you should stop and investigate as soon as possible. Leaking or spilling petrol can be dangerous because it is so combustible.
>
> It is good practice to carry a fire extinguisher in your vehicle, so that you can deal with any small fires.

Breakdowns

If your vehicle breaks down, you should make sure that it does not cause a hazard to other road users, and that any action you take does not put you or others in danger.

When should a driver use hazard warning lights on a motorway?

When the vehicle has broken down.

If your vehicle breaks down on a motorway, drive it to the hard shoulder and switch on the hazard warning lights to warn following traffic. When it is safe to do so, get out of the vehicle and move behind the barrier. Call for assistance from a motorway emergency phone or using a mobile phone (call the Gardaí).

What should a driver do if their vehicle is broken down and they are awaiting assistance?

Switch on the vehicle hazard warning lights, get out of the vehicle and stand to the side.

If your vehicle breaks down on the road, always switch on the hazard warning lights and stand clear of the vehicle while awaiting assistance – this will warn other traffic that there is a vehicle stopped on the road.

Meeting emergency or extra-large vehicles

It is important that you know how to react and respond when you meet emergency vehicles, such as fire brigades, ambulances and Garda cars, either coming towards you or coming up behind you. These vehicles are sometimes moving very fast, and you must get out of their way as quickly as you can, provided it is safe to do so.

What action should a driver take when they notice flashing blue lights in the rear-view mirror?

Move to the left, reduce speed and allow the vehicle to pass.

What action should a driver take when they meet a vehicle with flashing blue lights?

Move to the left, reduce speed and stop if necessary.

When you notice an emergency vehicle approaching, either from ahead or in your rear-view mirror, you should move in to the left where it is safe and allow the vehicle to pass safely. Avoid stopping immediately, as this could cause a greater obstruction to the emergency vehicle.

What should a driver do when they see road works machinery with amber flashing lights up ahead?

Slow down and prepare to stop if necessary.

When you notice works vehicles ahead, slow down and be prepared to stop for the road works. Be extra careful driving through road works as the road surface could be uneven or slippery.

What should a driver do if an ambulance is stopped up ahead with its flashing blue lights on?

Reduce speed and prepare to stop if necessary.

When you come upon an emergency vehicle stopped on the road, you should slow down and be prepared to stop. Do not stop to see what is happening as this could be dangerous and you might cause an obstruction to the flow of traffic.

How are emergency vehicles identified?

By flashing red or blue lights.

If you hear or see an emergency vehicle approaching sounding its siren or flashing lights, be extra careful and give way if it is safe to do so.

Which vehicle is exempt from speed limits when being used in an emergency?

Fire brigade.

Ambulance.

Garda.

In the course of their duty Garda, Fire Brigade and ambulance personnel are exempt from some traffic laws including speed limits, as long as they do not put other road users in danger. If you hear or see a Garda or emergency vehicle approaching under emergency conditions, be extra careful and give way, if it is safe to do so.

Part 2

Cars, light vans, tractors and works vehicles

Alert driving and showing consideration for other road users

While you are driving any motor vehicle, you must give your full attention to the task, and you must look out for other road users, some of whom may act in unexpected ways. The questions in this section check that you understand these issues.

What should a driver do when they want to use a mobile phone?

Pull in and stop in a safe place.

It is illegal to use a mobile phone while driving. Driving requires all of your attention, all of the time, so you should never use a mobile phone while on the road. If you want to use a mobile phone, you should find a safe place to stop.

When parked on a busy road, what should the driver be aware of?

Before opening the door the driver should make sure it is safe to do so.

When you park a vehicle on a busy road, make sure it is safe before opening the door, as there could be traffic passing close by.

In this situation, what should the driver in the right-hand lane of the dual carriageway be aware of?

Crosswinds may blow the rider into their path.

In wet and windy conditions, watch out for vulnerable road users being blown into your path.

What should a driver be aware of when queuing where there are multiple lanes of traffic?

Motorcycles or bicycles may come up on either side.

When you are queuing in traffic, use your mirrors, and watch out for vulnerable road users such as motorcyclists and cyclists passing on either side.

Seeing where you are going

As a driver, you must be able to see where you are going, and you must adjust the way you are driving to suit the road, weather and traffic conditions all around you. When you are going forward, you will mainly use your windscreen and mirrors for this; when you are reversing you will mainly be looking over your shoulder, while glancing around frequently.

Making sure that you can see properly

While you are driving any motor vehicle, you must have a clear view of the road ahead, and you must also be constantly aware of the road and traffic conditions around you to the sides and rear. The questions in this section check that you understand the importance of this, and that you know how to react if your view is obstructed in any way.

What should a driver do before towing a caravan?

Have extended mirrors fitted to the towing vehicle and use them regularly.

What should a driver do before towing a wide-bodied trailer?

Make use of extended mirrors to check for following traffic.

If you intend towing a trailer or caravan that is wider or higher than the vehicle that is towing it, you should fit extended mirrors to both sides of the towing vehicle, so that you will be able to assess the traffic situation behind and to the sides.

Why is it important to have clean, clear windows?

To ensure good all round visibility from the vehicle.

Make sure the windows of your vehicle are clear and clean at all times so that you can see road and traffic conditions around you. Dirty windows are particularly hazardous when the sun is low and at night.

If the vehicle's windows are covered with ice, what should the driver do before undertaking a journey?

Clear the ice from the windows before starting.

What should a driver do if the vehicle's windows are covered in ice?

Switch on the heating system and use a scraper to clear the ice before driving.

Make sure the windows of your vehicle are clear and clean at all times so that you can see road and traffic conditions around you. This is especially important when driving in slippery conditions. It is good practice to carry a can of de-icer in the vehicle and if possible to fill the washer reservoir with a de-icing agent.

What should a driver do if condensation is affecting the vehicle's windows?

Dry the windows with a cloth and then use the demister system.

Make sure the windows of your vehicle are clear and clean at all times so that you can see road and traffic conditions around you. Condensation on the window can seriously impair your ability to make proper observations.

How can sunlight affect visibility in a car with grimy windows?

It can create a mirror effect and reduce visibility.

Make sure the windows of your vehicle are clear and clean at all times so that you can see road and traffic conditions around you. Dirty windows are a particular hazard when the sun is low in the sky and at night.

Reversing

When you are reversing a vehicle, your ability to see where you are going and to see around the vehicle is restricted. For this reason, you must check carefully before you start, and execute the manoeuve slowly and carefully, checking all around you as you go. The questions in this section check your understanding of this issue.

What specific observations should a driver make before reversing their vehicle?

Look over both shoulders and behind.

Before reversing, look over both shoulders and to the rear to check that there are no children or other road users around the vehicle and that it is safe to reverse.

What specific observations should a driver make before reversing a vehicle fitted with an audible warning device?

Observations should be made to the front, sides and rear of the vehicle, including blind spots.

Before reversing, make sure it is safe to do so by taking all appropriate observations to the front, sides and rear of the vehicle, including the blindspots. Never assume it is safe to reverse just because the vehicle has an audible warning device.

What should a driver do when they intend to reverse onto a side road?

Check carefully all around before and during the reverse.

Before reversing onto a side road, check all around to make sure it is safe and clear to carry out the manoeuvre, paying particular attention to pedestrians crossing behind the vehicle and any other approaching traffic.

What should a driver do when they intend to reverse their vehicle on a busy street?

Reverse slowly, checking all around for other road users.

When reversing on a busy street, look all around and reverse slowly because there may be passing traffic and pedestrians attempting to cross the road.

What should a driver do if they intend to reverse their vehicle into an area which they cannot see?

Ask someone to assist when reversing.

Do not attempt to reverse into an area that you cannot see into properly, unless you get assistance from somebody who can advise you when it is safe to do so.

What should a driver do when reversing a vehicle with a trailer attached?

Look all around and use rear-view mirrors when reversing.

When reversing a vehicle with a trailer attached, make sure it is safe by checking all around and using the vehicle's mirrors. Reversing a vehicle with a trailer attached requires a lot of concentration, so watch out for other road users in the vicinity.

Remaining alert

Every driver has a responsibility to remain alert, and not to do anything that might impair their ability to react and respond to changes in the road or traffic conditions, or to the actions of other road users. Drivers should also be aware of the capabilities and limitations of the vehicle they are driving, and not drive in such a way that they endanger themselves or others.

What should a driver do in order to keep alert during a long journey?

Increase the air circulation and make regular stops if necessary.

While on a long journey, you should take regular rest breaks. A short walk and a caffeinated drink (tea or coffee) can help to revive you. Keep the vehicle cool and well ventilated with a steady flow of fresh air.

What would be the effect of a warm vehicle interior on somebody driving at night?

It could make the driver feel drowsy.

If you are driving at night in a vehicle with a high interior temperature, you can become drowsy. Keep the interior of the vehicle cool and well ventilated, and take regular breaks.

What effect would exhaust gases leaking into a vehicle have on the driver?

The driver may become drowsy or ill.

Exhaust gases leaking into a vehicle can make the driver drowsy or ill, and this can lead to a serious collision. If you suspect that exhaust gases are leaking into the vehicle, you should have it checked by a qualified person.

What in particular should a driver be aware of when driving a high-powered vehicle?

It could make the driver feel they are driving slower than they actually are.

When driving a smooth, high-powered vehicle, you may have the impression that you are travelling slower than you actually are. You should always know the speed at which you are driving, and adjust it as necessary to suit the road and traffic conditions.

Using the handbrake

Before you drive any vehicle, you must be familiar with its features and controls, and you must know how and when to use them. One of the most important features of any vehicle is its braking systems, and you must know when it is appropriate to use the foot brake and when to use the handbrake.

When should the handbrake be used to bring a vehicle to a halt?

Never.

The handbrake should never be used to bring a vehicle to a halt. This practice is potentially dangerous, as the rear wheels could lock up and the vehicle could skid out of control. In addition, using the handbrake does not operate the rear brake lights to warn following traffic.

What is the danger associated with applying the handbrake at speed?

The back wheels could lock and cause the vehicle to skid.

The handbrake should never be used when travelling at speed. This practice is potentially dangerous, as the rear wheels could lock up and the vehicle could skid out of control.

Driving on different road surfaces

You must modify your driving behaviour to take account of changes in the weather, the traffic conditions and the road surfaces. The questions in this section check that you know how to respond to different road surfaces.

In slippery conditions, should the driver of a tractor use the grass verge to improve road holding?

No, using the grass verge should be avoided.

You should not use the grass verge to gain traction on slippery roads. Hidden gulleys in the verge could cause you to lose control.

Why should a tractor be driven more slowly on uneven road surfaces?

To avoid severe bouncing.

Driving a tractor at speed on an uneven road surface could cause the vehicle or the trailer to become unstable and difficult to control.

Driving in fog

Driving in fog can be difficult, tiring and dangerous. Not only do you have difficulty in seeing the road markings and other traffic, but other road users also have difficulty in seeing you. The questions in this section check that you understand this issue and know how to respond.

When should rear fog lights be used?

In dense fog or falling snow.

When should high-intensity rear fog lights be used?

When driving in fog or falling snow.

You should use your rear fog lights only in fog or falling snow. Using fog lights in normal road and weather conditions can dazzle or blind following motorists. Also, fog lights may make your brake lights harder to see.

Driving at night

Driving at night, particularly along unlit roads or in wet weather, is challenging. You need to be sure that you can see the road ahead well enough, and that you can be seen by other road users.

What should a driver do if the right-hand headlight bulb fails when driving at night?

Have the bulb replaced immediately.

At night, what effect could driving with a single headlight have on oncoming drivers?

They could mistake the vehicle for a motorcycle.

Motor vehicles (except motorcycles) are required by law to have two headlights. Faulty lights should be repaired immediately. A vehicle with only one headlight could be mistaken for a motorcycle and other road users could believe that it is in a different position on the road than it actually is.

What should a driver do if dazzled by headlights reflecting in the rear-view mirror of their car?

Use the night driving mode on the mirror.

If the lights of following traffic are dazzling you, adjust your rear-view mirror to the night driving mode. This will allow you to concentrate on the road ahead and not be distracted by lights from following traffic.

What should a driver do if dazzled by lights reflecting in their exterior mirror?

Temporarily adjust the angle of the mirror.

If the lights of following traffic reflecting in your exterior mirror are dazzling you, temporarily adjust the angle of the mirror to relieve the glare and allow you to drive without distraction.

Generally, what lighting must a car, tractor or works vehicle have when driving at night?

Headlights, front and rear side lights, rear number plate light, red rear reflectors, brake lights and indicators.

> Cars, tractors and works vehicles are required by law to have headlights, front and rear side lights, rear number plate light, rear reflectors, brake lights and indicators.

What lights must be shown on a parked car, tractor or works vehicle at night on an unlit public road?

At least one side lamp front and rear on the side nearest the centre of the road.

> When leaving a vehicle on an unlit public road at night you should leave side/parking lights on, so that your vehicle can be seen by other road users.

Bridges and tunnels

Before going under a bridge or entering a tunnel, you must make sure that your vehicle will fit under it. You will see a advance warning sign before you come to the bridge or tunnel specifying the maximum height of vehicle that it can accommodate.

In addition, going over some bridges – in particular humpback bridges – poses a particular hazard for vehicles pulling a trailer, as there is a danger that the trailer may become detached from the towing vehicle.

What danger could be associated with driving a tractor and trailer over a humpbacked bridge?

The trailer could become detached.

> When towing a trailer, make sure that the tow hitch always has sufficient ground clearance. If this hits the road, for example when travelling over a humpbacked bridge, there is a danger that the trailer will become detached.

What should a driver do before entering a tunnel?

Check that the height of the vehicle is suitable for the tunnel.

What should a driver do before starting a journey on which they will encounter a tunnel?

Check the tunnel height before starting the journey.

You should know height of your vehicle and the load you are carrying, and plan your route accordingly. Always read the road ahead and watch for warning signs about height restrictions. These may relate to tunnels, low bridges or car park entrances.

Driving licences and learner permits

The questions in this section test that you know what the holder of each category of driving licence and learner permit is allowed and not allowed to do.

Where should L-plates be displayed on cars?

Both front and rear.

The holder of a learner permit must display L-plates on the front and rear of their car at all times when driving on public roads.

When must the holder of a learner permit display L-plates on their car?

At all times when driving.

The holder of a learner permit must display L-plates on the front and rear of their car at all times when driving on public roads.

How would a driver calculate the maximum permitted weight of their vehicle?

By adding the unladen weight of the vehicle to the load permitted to be carried.

The maximum permitted weight of a vehicle is the sum of the unladen weight of the vehicle and the maximum load that may be carried in it. It is an offence to overload a vehicle, as it reduces your ability to control it effectively.

What is the maximum gross weight of a vehicle that may be driven by the holder of a category B driving licence?

3,500 kilograms.

The holder of a category B driving licence is not permitted to drive a vehicle with a design gross vehicle weight of more than 3,500kgs. This restriction is noted on the licence.

What is the maximum number of passengers that may be carried in a vehicle driven by the holder of a category B driving licence?

8 passengers.

The holder of a category B driving licence is not permitted to drive a vehicle that has seating for more than 8 passengers excluding the driver.

When can the holder of a category W learner permit carry a passenger?

Only when the passenger also holds a category W driving licence and the vehicle is designed to take a passenger.

The holder of a category W learner permit may carry a passenger in the vehicle only if:
- The vehicle is designed to take a passenger, and
- The passenger has held a full driving licence in category W for two or more years.

Collisions and breakdowns

At the scene of a collision or breakdown, do not do anything that might make the situation worse. Make sure that any injured persons are properly attended to by contacting the emergency services. Make sure that oncoming traffic is given adequate warning of any hazard and that bystanders are not exposed to danger.

A driver has stalled in the middle of an unguarded level crossing and cannot restart the engine. The warning bell is ringing. What should the driver do?

Walk clear of the crossing and phone the signal operator so that trains can be stopped.

Get passengers clear of the crossing and phone the signal operator so that trains can be stopped.

In this situation, you and all passengers should get out of the vehicle and immediately use the emergency phone at the crossing to contact the signal operator so that trains can be stopped. If necessary, warn other motorists. Do not return to the vehicle until instructed by the signal operator or emergency services.

What is the immediate effect of a head-on collision between two cars at speed?

All persons in each vehicle are thrown violently forward.

In a head-on collision passengers in both vehicles are propelled forwards, and if they are not wearing seatbelts they may go through the windscreen. It is the driver's responsibility to ensure that all passengers under the age of 17 wear seatbelts. Older passengers are themselves responsible for wearing seatbelts.

When changing a wheel on a public road, what should a person do to ensure their their own safety?

Wear reflective clothing and switch on the vehicle hazard warning lights.

When changing a wheel at the side of the road, switch on the vehicle hazard warning lights, and wear reflective or light-coloured clothing. This will help other motorists to react and slow down when passing.

Carrying passengers

The questions in this section check that you know the regulations relating to carrying passengers, and that you know how to drive and operate your vehicle in a way that ensures the comfort and safety of the passengers.

Why is it dangerous to allow children to stand in the space between the front seats of a car?

They could be thrown forward if the brakes are applied suddenly.

When are children allowed to stand with their heads up through an open sun roof?

Children are never allowed to do so.

When carrying children in a car or goods vehicle, it is the driver's responsibility to make sure that they are suitably restrained.

Are children allowed to be left unattended in a vehicle?

Children should never be left unattended in a vehicle.

Children must not be left unattended in a vehicle, even for a short period of time. Children might interfere with the vehicle's controls, and would not be able to deal with an emergency situation, such as a fire or electrical malfunction which could result in serious injury or death.

When is a driver allowed to carry more passengers in a car than there are seatbelts available?

It is never allowed.

A driver must make sure that each passenger in the vehicle has a seatbelt. Failure to wear a seatbelt is an offence.

It is the driver's responsibility to ensure that passengers under the age of 17 wear seatbelts. Older passengers are themselves responsible for wearing seatbelts.

Safety on tractors

The questions in this section check that you understand the dangers of working in or around tractors.

When should children be allowed to drive a tractor?

Children should never be allowed to drive a tractor.

Persons under 16 years of age are not permitted to drive a tractor in a public place.

What danger can arise from the power take-off shaft of a tractor?

If it is not covered, clothing can get caught in it.

If you are working at the rear of a tractor, you should bear in mind that if the power take-off shaft is not covered, loose clothing might get caught in it and lead to injury or death.

Carrying loads

The questions in this section check that you know the dangers associated with carrying a load in your vehicle, and that you know how to do so safely.

When is a red flag a sufficient marker for a rear load overhang that exceeds one metre?

Only during the day.

During daylight hours, you must use a red flag to mark any load that is protruding more than one metre. At night, you must use a red light.

How should a driver negotiate a bend when driving a fully loaded vehicle?

At a slower speed than when empty.

Driving too fast on the approach to a bend and while driving through it with a fully loaded vehicle can lead to a loss of control. This can be prevented by driving in a safe and sensible manner and by reading the road ahead.

What should a driver do when requested to drive a vehicle that they feel is overloaded?

Refuse to drive the vehicle.

You should not take a vehicle that you believe to be overloaded onto a public road. Overloading is dangerous, as it affects the stability and braking capabilities of the vehicle.

How could towing an overloaded trailer affect a vehicle?

It could impair the vehicle's steering and braking.

You should not take an overloaded trailer onto a public road. An overloaded trailer impairs the stability, steering and braking of the towing vehicle.

At what point is a vehicle load more likely to shift?

When cornering.

It is the driver's responsibility to ensure that the load is properly secured and evenly distributed, so that the vehicle can be properly controlled when changing direction and when braking.

Towing a trailer

The questions in this section check that you know how to tow a trailer safely.

When attaching a trailer to their vehicle, what should a driver check?

That the load is evenly spread.

Proper weight distribution helps to ensure the stability of both the towing vehicle and the trailer. In the trailer, the bulk of the load should be over the axles. If a heavy load is positioned at the front of the trailer, this will result in too much 'nose weight' on the hitch of the towing vehicle and make it difficult to steer. If a heavy load is positioned at the rear of the trailer, this will result in reduced weight on the rear axle of the towing vehicle, which will make it more unstable.

When attaching a trailer to their vehicle, what should a driver check?

That the trailer coupling is attached securely.

Before towing a trailer or a caravan, check that the towbar is securely attached to the towing vehicle, that the trailer coupling is properly attached to the towbar and locked in place, and that the breakaway cable is properly connected.

What should a driver do before unhitching a trailer from a towing vehicle?

Apply the handbrake, switch off the ignition and engage a low gear.

Before unhitching a trailer, apply the handbrake, switch off the ignition and engage a lower gear, so that the towing vehicle does not move while you are unhitching the trailer.

When is it permissible for a driver to carry a passenger on a trailer drawbar?

Never.

You must never carry a passenger on a trailer drawbar because of the danger of the passenger falling between the vehicle and the trailer and being seriously injured or killed.

When is a tractor most likely to overturn?

When turning sharply.

Tractors are less stable than other vehicles as they have no suspension and the extra height and uneven positioning of the wheels adds to the instability. When you are driving a tractor, you should take these factors into account and take extra care when manoeuvring.

When driving a tractor and trailer, what should the driver do on entering a roundabout to avoid possible roll-over?

Reduce speed.

When you are driving a tractor with a trailer, you need to take extra care because of the vehicle's instability. Always drive at a safe speed, in particular when changing direction, such as on a roundabout.

What is jack-knifing?

When the trailer is travelling faster than the drawing vehicle.

When is jack-knifing most likely to occur?

When trying to reduce speed sharply while travelling downhill.

Towing a trailer or caravan dramatically reduces the stability of the towing vehicle. If a driver brakes sharply or slows down quickly, the trailer may pivot around the tow hitch coupling, causing both vehicles to go off course, and possibly overturn.

The driver of a tractor pulling a wide load that blocks their view to the rear wishes to turn right. What should they do?

Have another person advise of following traffic while the driver checks for oncoming traffic.

If you are driving a vehicle with a wide load that blocks your view of the road to the rear, and you need to turn right, you should get someone else to look out to the rear and advise you when it is safe to make the turn.

Technical matters with a bearing on road safety

The questions in this section check that you know how to keep your vehicle in good condition, that you recognise signs that it needs to be repaired or serviced, and that you understand the implications for your own safety and that of others of driving a vehicle in poor condition.

Side lights

The primary purpose of side lights is to make the vehicle more visible when it is parked. Don't use them when driving at night – use dipped headlights instead.

When should a driver use the vehicle side lights?

When parking on an unlit road.

You should use the side lights of your vehicle when parking on an unlit road at night, so that the vehicle can be easily seen by other road users.

How does a driver know if the bulb in a side light has failed?

By checking the side lights when they are switched on.

You must ensure that the lights in your vehicle are working properly before driving on the road. Check all the vehicle lights regularly by switching them on and getting out of the vehicle to see if they are working, or by getting someone else to check for you.

Dashboard warning lights

Modern engines are equipped with sophisticated systems for monitoring the condition of the engine and other parts of the vehicle, and for warning the driver if something goes wrong. These warnings are generally in the form of a warning light on the dashboard.

What does this warning light indicate?

A fault in the braking system.

If the brake warning light is on, there is a problem with the braking system in the vehicle or the handbrake is on. You should not drive the vehicle until the problem has been rectified.

Lights on trailers

If you are towing a trailer, it must have a rear number plate. The lighting requirements are similar to those for the towing vehicle. These questions check that you know these requirements.

What lighting should be on a car-trailer?

What lighting should be on a tractor-trailer during lighting-up hours?

Indicators, brake lights, rear number plate light, red reflectors and rear tail lights.

> All vehicles, including trailers, must have rear indicators, brake lights, a rear number plate light, red reflectors and rear tail lights.

Hazard warning lights

Your hazard warning lights are an important way of communicating to other road users that there is a danger on the road ahead. You should know when and how to use them.

On a motorway, when should a driver use the hazard warning lights?

When slowing down quickly because of danger ahead.

When the vehicle has broken down.

When should a driver use their hazard warning lights?

When the vehicle has broken down.

When causing an unavoidable obstruction.

What does using the vehicle's hazard warning lights allow a driver to do?

To warn other road users that the vehicle is broken down.

What effect do the hazard warning lights have on the brake lights?

They have no effect.

> Use the hazard warning lights to warn other road users of a danger ahead. For example, you can use the hazard warning lights to warn following vehicles of your presence in these situations:
>
> - If you have to slow down sharply – for example, because of a build-up of traffic ahead; or
> - if your vehicle has broken down and is causing an obstruction or is stopped on the hard shoulder.
>
> Hazard warning lights work independently of all other vehicle lights (except direction indicators), and using them has no effect on the brake lights.

Brakes

Before you drive any vehicle, you must be familiar with its features and controls, and you must know how and when to use them. One of the most important features of any vehicle is its braking systems, and you must know when it is appropriate to use the foot brake and when to use the handbrake.

The handbrake generally works on which wheels?

The rear wheels.

The function of the handbrake (or 'parking brake') is to stop the vehicle from moving when it is parked or when it is stopped on a hill. You normally use the handbrake when the vehicle is already stationary – you don't use it to stop the vehicle.

In vehicles with automatic transmission, use the handbrake when stationary to prevent 'creep'.

In most vehicles, the handbrake operates on the rear wheels only.

In general, above what gross vehicle weight must a trailer have brakes fitted?

750 kg.

Brakes must be fitted to a trailer if its gross vehicle weight exceeds 750kg or half the weight of the towing vehicle.

Driving a vehicle with automatic transmission

A vehicle with automatic transmission has some obvious differences from one with manual transmission (such as no clutch), and some differences that are not so obvious. You need to be aware of these differences, particularly if you sometimes drive a manual vehicle and sometimes an automatic.

What is the recommended method of driving a vehicle with automatic transmission?

Operate the accelerator and brake with the right foot.

When driving an automatic vehicle, you should use the right foot to operate both the accelerator and the brake, just as in vehicles with a manual gear box.

Fuel and oil

The oil in your engine lubricates and cools the moving parts of the engine. If there is too little oil in the engine, or if it is not reaching the parts that need it, the engine can be permanently damaged. Over-filling the engine with oil also causes problems.

If you are driving a diesel engined car, you must always use unrebated (white) diesel in it, rather than green diesel.

When driving a vehicle with a diesel engine in freezing weather, what should a driver ensure?

That the fuel is treated with an anti-waxing agent.

Road diesel is supplied with an anti-waxing agent added to it. This generally prevents the fuel from freezing at temperatures as low as -15°C.

What is a possible effect of over-filling the engine with oil?

It could damage the catalytic converter.

Catalytic converters are part of most vehicles' exhaust system. They remove up to 75% of the carbon monoxide, nitrogen oxide and hydrocarbons from the vehicles' exhaust. Catalytic converters can be permanently damaged if, for example, the car is filled with leaded petrol rather than unleaded, or if the engine is over-filled with oil.

What should a driver do if the fuel system becomes air-locked?

Bleed the air out of the fuel system.

The fuel system can become air-locked if you let the fuel get too low or if there is a leak in the system. You should have the problem corrected before driving. The solution may be as simple as bleeding the fuel system to release the air.

Is a driver allowed to use rebated (green) diesel fuel in a car on a public road?

Green diesel may never be used in a car.

If, in its normal use, a vehicle is used on a public road, it must use unrebated (white) diesel, as the appropriate excise duties are included in the purchase price. You can be prosecuted for using green diesel in a vehicle on a public road.

Head restraints

What should a driver do to reduce the risk of neck injury in a rear-end collision?

Use a properly adjusted head restraint.

Head restraints are designed to protect the neck and spine in a collision and thus prevent or reduce whiplash. They should be properly adjusted for both the driver and the passengers.

Rear-view mirror on tractors

When must a tractor or works vehicle be fitted with a rear-view mirror?

A rear-view mirror must always be fitted.

All vehicles used on a public road must have a rear-view mirror to enable the driver to see road and traffic conditions behind and to each side.

Tyres

Your ability to control your vehicle, to steer it in the direction you want and to stop it when and where you want depends critically on the few square centimetres of rubber that are in contact with the road at any time. You must make sure that your tyres are in good condition and correctly inflated.

What is the minimum legal tread depth for tyres on cars?

1.6 millimetres.

All road vehicles, except motorcycles and vintage vehicles, must have a minimum tyre tread depth of 1.6mm over the main tread. However, for safety reasons, you should replace the vehicle's tyres before they become this worn.

What does the load index of a tyre indicate?

The maximum load a tyre can carry.

The load index indicates the maximum weight that a tyre can support safely. When replacing a tyre on your vehicle, you should make sure that the new tyre maintains the proper load index for the vehicle.

Under what circumstances could both cross-ply and radial tyres be fitted to a vehicle?

When each type is fitted on a different axle.

In general, you should fit the same type of tyres all round the vehicle. However if you need to fit a mix of cross-ply and radials, the tyres on any axle should be of the same type.

Clutch

What is the effect of resting the foot on the clutch pedal?

It wears out the clutch more quickly than normal.

The clutch is the connection between the engine and the gearbox. It enables the vehicle to move when a gear is engaged. When driving, you should not rest your foot on the clutch pedal, because it might disengage the selected gear and/or damage the clutch mechanism.

Side-impact protection bars

What is the purpose of side-impact protection bars?

To protect the occupants when the vehicle is hit from the side.

Side-impact protection bars are fitted to some vehicles to protect the occupants of the vehicle in the event of a collision from the side.

Power-assisted steering

Power-assisted steering depends on a hydraulic system that includes a fluid reservoir. This reservoir should be kept filled in accordance with the manufacturer's instructions.

When the fluid reservoir is full to the mark, how would a driver check that the power-assisted steering is working effectively?

Turn the steering wheel from lock to lock with the engine running.

Before starting a journey, check that the PAS (power-assisted steering) is working by starting the engine and turning the steering wheel from full left lock to full right lock, to see that it operates smoothly and effectively.

What should the driver of a vehicle with power-assisted steering (PAS) do if steering becomes more difficult as they are driving?

Stop, check the level of the fluid and top up if necessary.

Most modern vehicles have power-assisted steering (PAS). PAS requires less effort and feels lighter, especially when carrying out manoeuvres such as parking, U-turns and reversing. You should be aware that it is easy to oversteer with PAS.

Seats

What is the effect of an incorrectly adjusted driver's seat?

It can delay the driver from operating a control.

Before starting a journey, you should adopt a suitable and comfortable driving position by adjusting the driver's seat to a position where all the vehicle controls can be operated efficiently.

Windscreen wipers and washer

You have to keep your windscreen clean and clear in order to see the road ahead and the traffic conditions around you, Your windscreen wipers and washer are essential pieces of equipment for this purpose, and you must know how to keep them in good condition.

While driving in rain, a driver notices that the wiper blades are worn. What should they do?

Have the blades replaced as soon as possible.

What should a driver do when the wiper blade on the driver's side is partly worn?

Have the worn blade replaced with a new one.

Use the windscreen wipers to keep the windscreen clear of rain, spray, snow or fog. Check them regularly to ensure that they are in good working order, and replace them when they become worn, before they become ineffective.

If the wiper blades are frozen to the windscreen, what should the driver do?

Defrost the windscreen before switching on the wipers.

Before starting a journey in icy weather, make sure that the windows are clear. Use the demister to clear the windows and defrost the wipers so that they can be used to clear the windscreen.

What problem is indicated when wipers suddenly cease to function?

A fuse has blown.

Check the vehicle's windscreen wipers regularly to ensure the blades are in good condition, and check that there is water in the washer bottle. If the wipers stop working suddenly, the most likely cause is a blown fuse.

What should a driver add to windscreen washer fluid in freezing weather?

A mild anti-freezing agent for windows.

In cold weather, use an anti-freezing agent in the windscreen washer fluid, so that the windscreen can be cleared if required.

Why is a windscreen laminated?

So as not to shatter into large fragments when struck by an object.

A laminated windscreen (a plastic film sandwiched between two layers of glass) is designed not to break into large fragments when struck by an object. This is to prevent serious injury to the driver and passengers.

Changing a wheel

The questions in this section check that you know how to change a wheel on a car safely.

When replacing a wheel, how should wheel nuts be tightened?

Diagonally.

When fitting a wheel to your vehicle, tighten the nuts gradually and evenly by tightening them 'diagonally'. For example, if the wheel has four nuts, first tighten the two nuts along one diagonal, then tighten the nuts on the other diagonal. If the wheel has five nuts, tighten each alternate nut until all are tightened. All nuts should be tightened to the manufacturer's recommended torque.

When changing a wheel on their vehicle on a public road, what should a person do?

Turn on the hazard warning lights.

Place a red warning triangle to the right side at the rear of the vehicle.

Wear reflective clothing if available.

When changing a wheel on a public road, make yourself as visible as possible. Wear high-visibility outer clothing, turn on the hazard warning lights, and place a red warning triangle to the rear of the vehicle on the right-hand side.

Environmental matters

Motor vehicles are a significant cause of pollution. In particular, they generate large amounts of the gases that are causing climate change. Other environmental effects include the amount of noise generated by engines and tyres.

All drivers should be aware of these effects, and modify their driving habits to minimise their negative impact on the environment. The questions in this section check that you understand the issues involved and that you know how to drive responsibly.

What should a driver do in order to avoid excessive exhaust pollution from their vehicle?

Have the vehicle's air filters changed regularly.

You should have your vehicle serviced regularly in accordance with the manufacturer's guidelines. A vehicle that is poorly tuned uses more fuel and creates more exhaust pollution. Air filters should be changed as part of normal servicing. If a vehicle is used in dusty conditions, the air filter may need to be changed more often. More information is available in the vehicle owner's handbook.

How regularly should a vehicle be serviced?

As often as indicated in the manufacturer's specification.

You should have your vehicle serviced regularly in accordance with the manufacturer's guidelines. This helps the vehicle to perform properly, thus saving fuel and reducing emissions. You should also carry out your own daily and weekly checks on fluid levels and tyres.

What is the purpose of a catalytic converter?

To reduce harmful exhaust emissions.

Catalytic converters are part of most vehicles' exhaust system. They remove up to 75% of the carbon monoxide, nitrogen oxide and hydrocarbons from the vehicles' exhaust.

What type of noise might fast cornering create?

Tyre squeal.

If you drive around a corner too fast, the tyres begin to lose contact with the surface of the road, and this causes a squealing sound. If you continue driving in this way, you can lose control of the vehicle.

Getting out of the vehicle

Before you get out of your vehicle, check that opening the door will not interfere with other road users, and that you can get out safely. Similarly, when you are letting passengers out, you must make sure that they can do so safely.

What should a driver do before getting out of the vehicle?

Check their side mirror and look behind before opening the door.

Check all around for approaching traffic and pedestrians before opening the door.

Before opening any door, check for other road users passing, and in particular look out for pedestrians, cyclists and motorcyclists. Exit the vehicle only when it is safe to do so, and close the door as soon as possible. Passengers should exit on the side nearest the kerb wherever possible.

How should a driver secure their vehicle before getting out of it?

Apply the parking brake, stop the engine and engage a low gear.

Before leaving your vehicle, apply the handbrake, switch off the engine and engage a low gear. If the vehicle is fitted with automatic transmission, select 'P' (park).

On a busy road, how should a driver allow passengers out of a vehicle?

Stop and allow them to get out on the side nearest the kerb.

Before allowing any door to be opened, check for other road users passing, and in particular look out for pedestrians, cyclists and motorcyclists. Passengers should exit on the side nearest the kerb, without getting in the way of pedestrians.

Seatbelts and child restraint systems

Any adult aged 17 years or over travelling in a car – whether in the front or the rear seat – is required to wear a seatbelt. Persons under the age of 17 who weigh more than 36 kg, or are more than 135 cm in height, must also wear adult seatbelts. Lighter, smaller children and babies must be restrained in special seats, harnesses or restraints. The questions in this section check that you know your responsibilities in this regard.

What cars are required to have rear seatbelts fitted?

Cars first registered after 1st January 1992.

Rear seatbelts are compulsory on all cars registered after 1st January 1992.

Where seatbelts are fitted to a car when must adult occupants wear them?

At all times.

The driver and all passengers in a car must wear a seatbelt or, in the case of a child, a suitable restraint system.

What is the purpose of a seatbelt?

To prevent the wearer from being thrown forward in the event of a crash or abrupt deceleration.

Seatbelts save lives and reduce the risk of injury by restraining the occupants of a vehicle in the event of a crash or sudden deceleration.

When should a driver put on their safety belt?

Before they move off.

Before moving off, put on your seatbelt and make sure that all your passengers also have theirs on.

Who is responsible for ensuring that a passenger over 17 years of age is wearing a seatbelt while travelling in a car?

The passenger only.

Who is responsible for ensuring that a passenger under 17 years of age is wearing a seatbelt while travelling in a car?

The driver only.

What should a driver do when driving a vehicle with young children as passengers?

Make sure each child is wearing a seatbelt or using an appropriate restraint system.

If the passenger is over the age of 17, it is their responsibility to comply with the seatbelt regulations. Below that age, it is the driver's responsibility.

In general, how should infants be secured in a vehicle?

They should always be secured in a child restraint system.

As safety belts are designed mainly for adults and older children, infants and small children must be restrained in an appropriate child restraint system.

Should an infant who is not secured in a child restraint system be carried in the front passenger seat?

No, an infant must always be restrained in a correct child seat.

Infants and small children must be restrained in an appropriate child restraint system.

How should a child restraint system be secured in a vehicle?

It should be secured with seatbelts or ISOFIX fittings.

A child restraint system should be secured in the vehicle either with the seatbelts of the car or with approved fixings. Always use a restraint system that is appropriate for the age, height and weight of the child, and follow the manufacturer's instructions.

Dealing with emergencies

The questions in this section deal with a number of emergency situations that you may find yourself in. They include getting a puncture while you are driving, skidding, breaking down, and avoiding a collision.

Punctures

A puncture is always an inconvenience, but it is also sometimes dangerous. If you get a sudden puncture while driving, you must know what to do in order to keep control of the vehicle and not endanger yourself or others.

What should a driver do if a tyre bursts on the vehicle they are driving?

Hold the steering wheel firmly and pull in on the side of the road.

What should a driver do if they get a tyre blow-out on the road?

Apply the footbrake gently and bring the vehicle to a halt.

> If a tyre bursts on your vehicle, keep a firm hold of the steering, slow down gradually and stop where it is safe to do so. Switch on your hazard warning lights and change the wheel or call for assistance.

What effect could a front-tyre blow-out have on a vehicle?

The steering wheel will pull to one side.

> If a front tyre on the vehicle you are driving blows out, you will feel the effect of it through the steering wheel. The wheel will generally pull to the side of the blown-out tyre.

What effect could a rear-tyre blow-out have on a vehicle?

It could cause the vehicle to sway from side to side.

> If a rear tyre on the vehicle you are driving blows out, the vehicle may sway from side to side, and this will affect its stability. Slow down, pull in where it is safe to do so, and switch on the hazard warning lights. Change the wheel or call for assistance.

Skidding

You should always drive in a way that is suited to the weather conditions and the state of the road. If you do, you will generally avoid skidding. However, if you do find yourself in a skid, you must know how to react in order to get the vehicle back into control as soon as possible. These questions check that you understand the causes of skidding and how to avoid them.

How should a driver use the brakes if the vehicle is fitted with anti-lock brakes (ABS)?

Press the brake pedal firmly and hold.

If your vehicle is fitted with ABS, brake firmly. ABS will not stop the vehicle more quickly, it will only prevent the wheels from locking. This helps you to maintain control of the vehicle.

What should a driver do if their vehicle gets into a four-wheel sideways skid?

Turn the steering wheel in the same direction as the skid and ease off the accelerator.

If your vehicle goes into a four-wheel skid, turn the steering wheel in the same direction as the skid and ease off the accelerator. This should help to bring the wheels back into line and allow you to regain control.

What should a driver do if their vehicle gets into a front-wheel sideways skid?

Release the accelerator.

If your vehicle goes into a front-wheel sideways skid, release the accelerator and do not try to steer until the tyres regain some grip on the road.

What should a driver do if their vehicle gets into a rear-wheel sideways skid?

Turn the steering wheel in the same direction as the rear wheels are heading.

If your vehicle goes into a rear-wheel sideways skid, turn the steering in the direction the rear wheels are heading. This should be done very gradually, as too much steering could cause the vehicle to skid in the opposite direction.

How should a driver in a vehicle without anti-lock brakes (ABS) deal with a front-wheel straight-line skid?

Press and release the footbrake at rapid intervals.

If your vehicle does not have ABS and it goes into a straight-line front-wheel skid due to braking, press and release the brake pedal repeatedly and rapidly. This will help to restore tyre grip and enable you to regain control.

Breakdowns and emergencies

If your vehicle breaks down, you should make sure that it does not cause a hazard to other road users, and that any action you take does not put you or others in danger. You must also know how to react and respond to emergency situations, and how to bring your vehicle to a stop quickly and safely.

What action should a driver take if the engine in their vehicle cuts out suddenly when they are driving along?

Signal and steer the vehicle to the side of the road.

If the engine in the vehicle you are driving cuts out, signal and steer to the side of the road. Switch on the hazard warning lights and contact the relevant breakdown service to get assistance.

How would hydraulic power steering be affected if an engine stalled in slow-moving traffic?

The steering would become heavy and difficult to operate.

Hydraulic power steering is operated by a pump which is driven by the engine. If the engine stalls, the pump stops working, and the steering becomes heavy and requires much more effort to turn.

What should a driver do if the accelerator jams when they are driving along?

Engage neutral gear and apply the brakes.

If the accelerator on the vehicle you are driving jams, select neutral and use the brakes to bring the vehicle to a safe halt. Switch off the engine as soon as the vehicle has stopped. Get the vehicle checked out before attempting to drive again.

When driving on the road, what should a driver do if the brakes on their vehicle fail?

Engage a lower gear.

Pump the brake pedal rapidly.

If the brakes on the vehicle fail while you are driving fail, select a lower gear to slow the vehicle down and move to the left to come to a halt.

You can also try to regain some braking by pumping the footbrake. This may help you to bring the vehicle to a safe stop.

When driving along, a driver feels that the oncoming car may crash into their vehicle. What should they do?

Flash the headlights and sound the horn to attract the attention of the other driver.

If there is an oncoming vehicle in your path, flash your lights and sound your horn to alert the other driver. Bring your vehicle to a halt immediately.

When driving along and confronted by an obstacle, what should a driver do?

When driving along and required to stop suddenly, what should a driver do?

When required to stop in an emergency, what should a driver do?

Apply the footbrake firmly.

Maintain firm pressure on the footbrake.

To stop your vehicle in an emergency, apply the footbrake firmly, and maintain the pressure until the vehicle stops. Depress the clutch pedal just before stopping. Vehicles are fitted with braking systems to stop the vehicle.

What should a driver do to avoid having to make an emergency stop?

Keep a safe distance from the vehicle in front.

Scan the road well ahead.

When driving in traffic, read the road ahead and keep a safe distance from the vehicle in front. Use the two-second rule to determine your safe distance from the vehicle in front.

Part 3

Motorcycles and mopeds

Safety issues of particular importance for motorcyclists

Before you ride a motorcycle, you must be well prepared. You must equip yourself with the appropriate protective clothing, and you must be thoroughly familiar with the features and controls on the bike you are riding.

Protection and clothing

The questions in this section relate to the ways in which you can protect yourself from injury in the event of a fall or other incident. Some of them relate to legal requirements and some to recommended good practice.

What should someone always wear while riding a motorcycle?

Gloves, boots, helmet and protective clothing.

What standard should a motorcyclist's protective clothing meet?

A standard certified by a CE mark, that is a European Union Standards Mark.

When should a motorcyclist wear protective clothing?

In all situations.

You should always wear appropriate clothing and a secure helmet when riding a motorcycle, on every journey, no matter how short. You should wear a reflective jacket to make you more visible to other road users. Motorcycle gloves, boots, helmets and protective clothing are designed to protect the wearer from adverse weather conditions and against injury in the event of a crash or fall. Motorcycle clothing that claims to give protection must be marked with a European Standard CE Mark.

What footwear should a motorcyclist wear while riding?

Protective boots.

You should wear secure and reinforced boots on every journey. Shoes, sandals or runners do not offer any protection from the weather or support in the event of a crash or fall. Boots should be high enough to protect your shins and support your ankles.

Why should someone wear gloves when riding a motorcycle?

To protect the motorcyclist's hands in the event of a fall.

Under what circumstances should a motorcyclist wear gloves?

At all times.

You should wear proper motorcycle gloves on every journey. These will protect your hands from the wind and rain, and help you to avoid injury in the event of a crash or fall. Choose gloves that offer maximum protection without hindering your ability to operate the controls easily.

How should a motorcyclist protect their eyes when riding a motorcycle?

By wearing a helmet with an adjustable visor.

You should always wear appropriate eye protection. Most helmets have an adjustable visor to protect the eyes from wind, rain, stone chippings, flies and insects. If the helmet does not have a visor, you should wear goggles.

When is it permitted to ride a motorcycle or moped on a public road without wearing a helmet?

Never.

You are legally required to wear a proper helmet while riding a moped or motorcycle in a public place. The helmet should meet EU standards and be securely fastened. It is illegal to wear an unsecured helmet, and an unsecured helmet is unlikely to be effective in the event of a crash.

Motorcycle features, taking care of the machine, safety

Modern motorcycles are complex machines. Before you take one onto the public road, you need to be totally familiar with all its features and controls, and know how to use them.

What does this light mean when displayed on the instrument panel?

A gear is not engaged.

The motorcycle is in neutral gear.

You should know and understand the various warning lights on the instrument panel. This green light tells you that a gear is not engaged. It is important to know this before starting the engine.

What does this switch operate?

Headlight.

This switch is used to alternate between dipped beam and main beam when riding at night. Motorcyclists should always travel with dipped headlight during the day.

On a motorcycle with manual transmission, what does this lever operate?

The clutch.

On a modern motorcycle with manual transmission, this lever is used to operate the clutch. It is used to disengage the drive between the engine and the driven wheel when moving away, stopping and changing gears.

What does this switch operate?

The emergency engine stop.

This switch operates the emergency engine stop or 'kill' switch. It should not normally be used to stop the engine except in emergency situations, such as after a crash or fall. However you should check it periodically to make sure that it is operating properly.

What does this lever operate?

The front brake.

On a modern motorcycle, this lever is used to operate the front brake. To apply the brake, you squeeze the lever. The harder you squeeze, the more pronounced is the braking effect. As the front brake is the most effective brake on the motorcycle, it should be used with care and precision when slowing or stopping.

Which fluid is contained in this reservoir?

Brake fluid.

Modern motorcycles fitted with hydraulic brakes normally have the front brake fluid reservoir mounted on the right-side handlebar. The reservoir can be either a clear container or one with a sight-glass to enable the fluid level to be checked. You should check this regularly with the motorcycle in an upright position on a level surface.

What does this foot lever, located on the nearside of a modern motorcycle, operate?

The gears.

On a modern motorcycle, the gear lever is located on the nearside (left side) just in front of the footrest. You select gears by lifting or pushing down the lever with your foot. You should familiarise yourself with your own motorcycle, as the number of gears varies with make and model.

What does this foot lever, located on the offside of a modern motorcycle, operate?

The foot brake.

On a modern motorcycle fitted with manual transmission, the rear brake lever is located on the offside (right side) in front of the footrest. You apply the rear brake by pressing the pedal with your foot. The rear brake is not as effective as the front, so you should use it in conjunction with the front brake for optimum stopping power.

What action should a motorcyclist take in the event of a front-wheel sideways skid?

Steer in the same direction that the motorcycle is heading and release the throttle.

In the event of a sideways skid, you should steer the motorcycle in the direction of the skid. Skids can be avoided by adjusting your speed to suit the road and traffic conditions.

What on a motorcycle should be checked weekly?

Petrol, oil, water, damage, electrics and tyres.

You should carry out a routine check on your motorcycle weekly. Checks should include petrol, oil, water, damage, electrics and rubber (tyres). If the bike is chain-driven, you should also check and lubricate the chain.

How should a motorcyclist take care of their motorcycle?

Visually inspect the motorcycle daily and carry out an inspection once a week.

A motorcycle in regular use should be checked daily, with a more detailed inspection once a week. Depending on the season and the usage of the motorcycle, these maintenance intervals may vary.

What is likely to happen if a motorcyclist fails to lubricate the drive chain on their motorcycle?

The rate of chain wear will increase.

You should inspect, lubricate and adjust your drive chain regularly, depending on your usage of the bike. Failure to lubricate the chain properly will increase the rate of wear dramatically. Special lubricants are available specifically for this purpose.

What could happen if the drive chain on a motorcycle is loose?

What might happen if a motorcycle is ridden while the drive chain is slack?

The rear wheel might lock

If a motorcycle chain is worn or loose, it could come off its sprockets and cause the rear wheel to lock, with a resultant loss of control.

What might happen if the drive chain of a motorcycle is incorrectly adjusted?

It could cause a rattling noise.

What could happen if a motorcycle is ridden with a worn drive chain?

The chain may stretch and become more noisy.

If a motorcycle chain is worn or loose, it could come off its sprockets and cause the rear wheel to lock, with a resultant loss of control. A worn chain will generally create a rattling noise, and this should prompt you to investigate and address the problem.

What should be checked after the drive chain has been adjusted?

Wheel alignment.

When you adjust the drive chain, you should make sure that the rear wheel is properly aligned. Otherwise the tyre may wear prematurely and the handling of the bike will be affected, especially during cornering.

What is the effect of applying the choke for a long period?

Increased fuel consumption and pollution.
The engine may run too fast.

What could happen if the choke is left on?

Engine wear and fuel consumption could increase.

The engine runs on a mixture of fuel and air. When the engine is cold, you should apply the choke to increase the amount of fuel in the mix. However, if you leave the choke on for longer than necessary, the idle speed of the engine will increase, which could make it more difficult to control the bike at lower speeds or when slowing or stopping. It will also lead to an increase in engine wear, fuel consumption and pollution.

What should a motorcyclist be aware of concerning cable-operated brakes?

That they stretch in use.

Cable-operated brakes should be inspected regularly to check that they are operating effectively. If the cable is frayed, it should be replaced, and if the brakes are not effective enough, the cable may need to be tightened.

In the interest of road safety, what should be kept clean on a motorcycle?

Headlight.

Number plate.

Rear lights.

Motorcyclists are responsible for keeping their motorcycles in good condition. Keeping the lights (front and rear), reflectors and number plate clean will increase your visibility to other road users.

What is a possible effect of incorrect wheel alignment on a motorcycle?

Reduced road holding.

Excessive tyre wear.

If the wheels are incorrectly aligned, the bike will run out of line. This will result in excessive or uneven tyre wear.

What is a possible cause of a badly aligned rear wheel?

Refitting the rear wheel.

When refitting a rear wheel to a motorcycle, you should make sure that it is aligned precisely behind the front wheel. Failure to do so could result in uneven tyre wear and/or instability when cornering.

What could happen if the steering head bearings are worn on a motorcycle?

The motorcycle could be difficult to control.

What would cause the steering to feel wobbly?

Worn steering head bearings.

The steering head bearings provide for smooth steering on a motorcycle. If they are worn, the steering becomes loose or wobbly, and the motorcycle becomes unstable. The bearings should be adjusted or replaced if necessary to restore smooth precise steering.

Under what circumstances should the engine cut-out switch be used?

In an emergency only.

You should use the engine cut-off switch only in an emergency, such as after a crash or a fall. However you should check it periodically to make sure that it is operating properly.

Why should a motorcyclist ensure the side stand is fully raised before moving away?

To avoid catching the ground and destabilising the motorcycle when cornering.

Use the side stand only for parking the motorcycle. Raise it fully before moving away. Riding with the side stand down is dangerous, as it may dig into the ground when cornering and cause you to lose control of the bike.

When should tyre pressures be increased?

When carrying a pillion passenger.

You may need to increase the tyre pressures on a motorcycle when carrying extra weight, such as a pillion passenger and / or luggage. Consult your owner's manual for the relevant tyre pressures.

What is the minimum legal tyre tread depth for motorcycles?

1.0 millimetres.

The minimum tyre tread depth for motorcycles is 1mm. However, it is advisable to replace the tyre before it wears that low to improve road holding, especially in wet weather. Some tyres have a wear indicator in the groove to show that the tyre is getting near to the minimum legal requirement.

What does the traction control system help to prevent?

Wheelspin when accelerating.

A traction control system on a motorcycle helps to prevent wheelspin when accelerating. This helps you to maximise the grip of the rear tyre when accelerating in slippery conditions, both when moving away and on bends and corners.

Riding your motorcycle

The questions in this section relate to the basic skills that you need to ride a motorcycle – starting and stopping the bike, moving off, adopting the appropriate position on the road, overtaking safely, taking emergency and corrective action and dealing with hazards.

Moving off

Moving off requires very fine control of the clutch lever, throttle and rear brake. Avoid jerky or sudden movements of the controls so that you don't jerk forward or cut out (stall). You also need to let each of your feet take your weight at different times. The questions below check that you understand these matters.

What should a motorcyclist check before starting the engine?

That the gear selector is in neutral.

> Before starting the engine, you should ensure that the gear selector is in neutral. This can be verified by checking that the green neutral light is showing on the instrument panel.

What should a motorcyclist do just before moving off from a parked position?

Look over their shoulder for a final glance.

What is a 'lifesaver look'?

A look over the shoulder just before moving off, turning or changing lanes.

When should a motorcyclist perform a 'lifesaver look'?

Before changing direction on a motorcycle.

> The final glance before moving away from the kerb or changing lanes is known as a 'lifesaver look'. A lifesaver look is a final look to the left, right or rear into the blind spot areas not covered by the mirrors. You should give a lifesaver look before moving off and before changing lanes or direction.

A motorcyclist in busy moving traffic wishes to change lanes. Why is a 'lifesaver look' required?

The mirror may not cover blind spots.

A 'lifesaver look' is a last look to the left, right or the rear into the blind spot areas not covered by the mirrors. You should give a lifesaver look before moving off and before changing direction.

Road position

For your own safety and the safety of other road users, it is important that you adopt the correct position on the road. Where lanes are not marked, you should keep to left, but not too close to the verge or to parked cars or the pavement. If the road is wet, you should avoid splashing pedestrians and cyclists. Where lanes are marked, you should adopt a position centrally between the lane markers. If you are going to turn off to the left or right, plan ahead, so that you are in the correct lane when you arrive at the junction.

In what position should a motorcyclist have their feet when stopped at traffic lights, STOP signs or in traffic?

The left foot down.

When stopped in traffic, you should have your left foot down to balance and your right foot on the rear brake to secure the motorcycle.

In what position should a motorcyclist have their feet when driving along in traffic?

Both feet up.

In order to maintain proper balance and control, you should always keep your feet on the foot rests while the motorcycle is in motion.

In this traffic situation, what is the position of the motorcyclist?

In the correct position.

In normal riding, what is the correct position on the road?

Mid-way between the near side and the centre of the road.

What is the main advantage of riding in the central position, midway between the near-side edge and the centre line of the road?

It gives the rider a good margin of safety on each side.

The normal position is in the centre of the lane. On a single carriageway road with two-way traffic, the correct position is half-way between the centre of the road and the left-hand side. The advantage of riding in this position is that you are more visible to other traffic, and you are in a better position to avoid potholes and road debris. It also reduces the potential for conflict with oncoming traffic. However, you should also take the width of the road, the condition of the road surface and any obstructions into consideration when riding.

On a single-track country road, what should a motorcyclist do?

Avoid the grass in the centre of the road.

When you are riding on a single-track country road, you should avoid the grass and debris that collects down the centre of the road, as this may cause instability and result in a fall.

What position should a motorcyclist take up behind a vehicle they are about to overtake?

The off-side of the vehicle in front.

When you intend to overtake the vehicle in front, you should position your bike to the off-side rear of the vehicle in front, leaving enough room to get a good view of the road ahead. You can then take the opportunity to overtake smoothly and safely.

When and why should a motorcyclist take up a near-side position?

When approaching a right-hand bend, to get an early view of the road ahead.

On approach to a right-hand bend with a restricted view ahead, what position should a motorcyclist adopt?

The near-side position.

When should a motorcyclist take up a near-side position?

In good time before turning left.

When approaching a right-hand bend with a restricted view of the road ahead, you should take up a position towards the left (near side) of the road, so as to gain a better view of the road ahead. This generally would apply outside of special speed limit areas.

You should also take up the near-side position before turning left. This prevents other traffic from passing on your inside and enables following traffic to continue ahead or to turn right in safety.

Under what circumstances should a motorcyclist take up an off-side position?

In good time before turning right.

What is the advantage of taking up an off-side position?

To get an early view through a left-hand bend.

When approaching a left-hand bend, you may position yourself towards the right of the lane, to give you a better view of the road ahead. This generally would apply outside of special speed limit areas.

You should also take up an off-side (right-side) position before turning right. This makes you more visible to other road users and allows following traffic to pass on your inside.

What position should a motorcyclist take up on approach to a left-hand bend?

The off-side position.

The off-side position gives a better view of the road ahead past a left-hand bend. You should, however, be aware of the possibility that oncoming vehicles may be straddling the centre of the road, in which case you should move more to the left.

What should a motorcyclist consider before taking up position on a left-hand bend?

Whether or not oncoming traffic requires a margin of safety.

Whether it is really necessary to alter course if their view ahead is unrestricted.

When riding in an urban area, what should a motorcyclist consider before taking up position on a left-hand bend?

Whether their position on the road might mislead other traffic into thinking that they intend to turn right.

When approaching a left-hand bend, you should consider whether taking up the off-side position is necessary. If there is an unrestricted view of the road ahead, it may be better to maintain your central position while going through the bend. In an urban area, you should be sure that your position will not mislead other road users. If following traffic believes that you are about to turn right, they may attempt to overtake you on your inside.

What is the advantage of correct positioning while cornering?

It gives an earlier and more extended view of the road ahead.

The advantage of taking up the correct position while cornering is that it gives you an early view of the road ahead through the bend. On left-hand bends it offers increased safety margins from hazards at the side of the road, and on right-hand bends it offers increased safety margins from oncoming traffic.

When a motorcyclist is cornering, what should they do?

Lean in the direction of the turn.

When you are cornering, you should lean towards the inside of the bend or curve. In this position, the force of gravity works to keep the bike stable. If you do not lean the bike into the curve or bend, its tendency is to continue in a straight line.

What effect does cornering at speed have on a motorcycle?

The motorcycle is less stable.

Extra demands are placed on tyre grip.

Cornering at speed reduces the stability of the bike and places extra demands on tyre grip. These effects increase with the severity of the bend, and the speed and weight of the bike.

How should a motorcyclist approach a bend?

At the correct speed.

In the correct position.

In the correct gear.

When approaching a bend, you should take up the correct position on the road, adjust your speed and select the appropriate gear for that speed. Going through the bend, you should maintain your line and a constant speed, in order to ensure stability and maximum tyre grip. This is especially important on a road that is uneven or wet.

What should a motorcyclist ensure during cornering?

That the speed is correct.

When cornering, you should maintain a constant and correct speed to ensure stability and maximum tyre grip. This is especially important on a road that is uneven or wet.

What should a motorcyclist allow for when negotiating a bend?

A change to poor road conditions.

Blind junctions or exits.

When cornering, you should expect the unexpected. A change in road conditions, such as potholes or mud on the road, or the emergence of other traffic from an exit, could lead to an incident.

How should a motorcyclist gauge the severity of a bend?

By noting where the near-side and off-side verges appear to meet and how this changes on approach.

Most bends and corners are marked with yellow warning signs. As you enter the bend, take note of the point at which the near-side verge and the off-side verge appear to meet, and note how this point changes as you proceed through the bend. This allows you to gauge the severity of the bend and adjust your speed as required.

Why is special care required when taking bends on a motorcycle with a sidecar attached?

The sidecar compartment cannot be leaned over.

Special care is needed when riding a motorcycle with a sidecar attached. This is particularly the case on bends and when turning – you cannot lean the unit in the way you can with a solo motorcycle, and the unit needs to be steered with a deliberate push or pull on the handlebars. This requires considerably more effort than leaning.

Why is special care required when taking a left-hand bend on a motorcycle with a sidecar attached?

The weight being thrown outwards will tend to lift the sidecar off the road.

Special care is needed when riding a motorcycle with a sidecar attached, especially when taking a left-hand bend, as the weight being thrown outwards tends to lift the sidecar off the road.

When riding in wet weather, what in particular should a motorcyclist be aware of?

That oil or diesel may gather on parts of the road.

When riding in wet weather, you should watch out for oil and/or diesel spillages. These can be identified by a rainbow-coloured film on the road. Avoid such areas if possible, as they are particularly dangerous for motorcyclists.

Overtaking

The ability to overtake slower-moving vehicles safely is one you need to develop. You should always be extremely careful when overtaking on the open road and should always ask yourself these questions: Is it necessary? Is it legal? and Is it safe? Remember that on a bike you are not as visible to other road users as larger vehicles, such as cars, trucks and buses.

What should a motorcyclist avoid when overtaking?

Causing oncoming traffic to alter course or speed.

Causing traffic being overtaken to alter course or speed.

Being unable to move back to the near side in plenty of time.

Before overtaking another vehicle, you should make sure that the road ahead is clear and that you can overtake safely without causing oncoming traffic or the traffic being overtaken to alter their speed or course. You should also allow sufficient clearance to the traffic being overtaken in case they alter course during the manoeuvre.

What should a motorcyclist avoid when overtaking on a single carriageway road with two-way traffic?

Making a third line of vehicles abreast.

When you are overtaking another vehicle on a single carriageway road with two-way traffic, you must not make a third lane abreast either by overtaking a vehicle that is itself already overtaking or by overtaking a vehicle when there is oncoming traffic, even if you do not cross the centre line of the road.

A motorcyclist is travelling in a near-side position behind a truck and wishes to take up an off-side position. What should they be aware of?

That areas of the road ahead will be lost from view while they are changing position.

If, while following a large vehicle, you change from a near-side position to an off-side position, your view of the road ahead will be greatly reduced while you are making the change, and your ability to see bends and other hazards will be reduced.

When overtaking a slow-moving truck, what hazard might arise?

The truck might turn right with late or no signal.

A slow-moving vehicle might be turning left onto the road up ahead.

The driver of a vehicle on a road to your left up ahead is turning right and is unaware of your presence.

The driver of a vehicle turning left from a junction on the right up ahead might have taken observations only to their right.

When you are preparing to overtake a slow-moving truck or large vehicle, there are many things to be aware of as a motorcyclist. You need to be aware not only of the vehicle ahead but also of other situations that may develop. Other road users may do something unexpected and may not always be as aware as they should be of a rider's presence.

Having just overtaken a large vehicle on a dual carriageway or motorway what should a motorcyclist do before moving back into the left-hand lane?

What should a motorcyclist do after overtaking a large vehicle on a dual carriageway?

Check the left-hand mirror, signal, and move in to the left when it is safe to do so.

After overtaking a large vehicle, you should check your left-hand mirror, signal, give a lifesaver look to the left and gradually move back into the left-hand lane without cutting across the vehicle you have overtaken.

A motorcyclist has moved closer to the vehicle in front prior to overtaking it. What should they be most aware of?

The driver in front may brake suddenly.

The driver in front may reduce speed.

The driver in front may accelerate suddenly.

As you approach the vehicle in front prior to overtaking it, you should be aware that you will have less time to react if the driver in front accelerates, slows or brakes suddenly. You should therefore assess all the hazards on the road ahead before taking up this position, and if the overtaking opportunity does not arise you should fall back to a safe following distance.

Taking emergency/corrective action

When riding a bike, you need to always expect the unexpected. You literally don't know what's around the next bend, but you can avoid some dangerous situations by developing your observation skills and learning to anticipate danger. Even the best and safest motorcyclists, however, will have to make emergency stops from time to time. The quicker you respond to a potential emergency, the more likely you are to avert it. So, keep alert and be ready.

What should a motorcyclist do if they get a sudden and severe puncture while riding?

Close the throttle and ease to a stop.

If you get a sudden and severe puncture while riding along, you should not brake suddenly as this would cause the bike to become more unstable. You should hold the handlebars firmly, ease off the throttle, and gradually bring the bike to a safe stop at the side of the road.

How should a motorcyclist normally stop their engine?

Turn off the ignition.

The normal sequence in stopping a motorcycle engine is as follows:
1. Close the throttle.
2. Engage neutral.
3. Switch off the engine using the ignition key.
4. Switch off the fuel tap (if fitted).

If you use the ignition key to stop the engine, you are less likely to leave the key in the ignition when leaving the motorcycle.

The emergency engine stop switch should be used only in an emergency.

How should a motorcyclist apply the brakes to stop quickly in an emergency?

Use the front brake followed by the rear brake.

When braking in an emergency, you should close the throttle and apply the front brake just before the rear, and increase the brake pressure steadily. You should consider the road and weather conditions, and apply the right amount of braking to each wheel to achieve maximum effort without causing the wheels to lock up and skid.

What should a motorcyclist do if their motorcycle engine cuts out while they are riding along?

Signal and steer the motorcycle to the side of the road.

If you are riding along and your motorcycle engine cuts out, you should check behind, signal and steer to the side of the road as soon as possible.

What action should a motorcyclist take in the event of a front-wheel sideways skid?

Turn the steering in the same direction as the motorcycle is heading and roll off the throttle.

What action should a motorcyclist take in the event of a rear-wheel sideways skid?

Turn the steering in the same direction as the rear wheel is heading and roll off the throttle.

In the event of a sideways skid, you should steer the bike in the direction of the skid. You should release the throttle or the brake, whichever is causing the skid. You can avoid skidding by adjusting your speed to suit the road, weather and traffic conditions.

Dealing with hazards

A hazard is anything that means you might have to change the position, speed, or direction of your motorcycle. For example, a road feature such as a sharp bend could be a hazard, and so could the actions of other road users.

As you become more experienced as a motorcyclist and build up experience of road and traffic conditions, you will become better at scanning the road ahead to anticipate and react to the different kinds of hazard that you meet. This will help you to further develop the essential skills of observation, judgement, planning and reaction.

What should a motorcyclist do when meeting a large vehicle on a narrow road?

Slow down and proceed with caution.

What should a motorcyclist be aware of when meeting a large vehicle on a narrow road?

Forward visibility is reduced.

If you meet a large vehicle on a narrow road, you should slow down and move to the left, provided it is safe to do so. You should also be prepared for other vehicles that may be hidden behind the approaching vehicle.

What hazard should a motorcyclist be aware of in this situation?

Wet road surface.

You should exercise caution when travelling on wet roads. Allow extra time for slowing or stopping, as tyre grip will be reduced. Take extra care when braking or cornering on wet surfaces.

In this situation, what does the motorcyclist need to consider?

They might be blown off course by wind turbulence from the oncoming truck.

When riding in the off-side position, you should be aware of any oncoming vehicles, especially those travelling near or over the centre of the road. You should also be prepared for wind turbulence created by large vehicles coming towards you at high speed.

What should a motorcyclist be aware of on approaching a railway crossing?

The barrier may come down.

The tracks may not be flush with the road.

Motorcyclists should approach crossings with caution. They should reduce speed and be prepared to stop if necessary. Be alert to changes in the road surface. The rails may not be at the same level as the road. Also the rails and road markings may be slippery in wet conditions.

Weather conditions

On a motorcycle, you are much more exposed to the weather than drivers of cars or trucks, and you are much more likely to be destabilised or put off course by bad weather. Any kind of weather that makes it more difficult for you to see what's happening on the road (and makes it more difficult for other road users to see you) presents particular riding challenges, especially while you are learning. Rain, fog, snow, ice, high winds, and even bright sunshine can present hazards that you must be prepared for. The questions in this section deal with your ability to meet these challenges.

What should a motorcyclist do while riding through a flood?

Keep the engine running fast.

Approach flooded areas with caution. If the flood water seems too deep, consider an alternative route. If it is not too deep, ride through in a low gear and keep the engine running fast in order to prevent water entering the exhaust.

Having gone through floods, how would a motorcyclist dry the brakes?

Drive slowly while applying the brakes briefly.

After riding through a flooded area, test your brakes immediately. The brakes can be dried by gently applying them a few times until normal braking is restored.

What should a motorcyclist be aware of when there is melting tar on the road?

Melting tar reduces tyre grip.

In hot weather what can be made worse by soft tar on the road?

Braking.

In very hot weather, tarmac road surfaces can become soft. When this happens, you should take extra care when braking and cornering, as tyre grip will be reduced.

What should motorcyclists do when riding in windy conditions?

Look ahead and anticipate crosswinds.

In strong winds, you can become more vulnerable on a motorcycle. Slow down and try to anticipate where crosswinds are most likely to affect you, such as when passing gaps in roadside hedges or between tall buildings, or on exposed roads and high bridges or flyovers. Be aware that the winds might also affect other road users, such as pedestrians, cyclists and high-sided vehicles.

How would a motorcyclist know if there was black ice on the road?

Tyre noise will decrease.

Black ice occurs when moisture freezes on a very cold surface. Exposed roads and bridges can have black ice when other sections of the same road may be clear. Black ice is virtually invisible, and so presents a particular hazard for motorcyclists. In wintry conditions, if you notice a reduction in tyre noise or if the steering becomes lighter, you should suspect that there may be black ice on the road.

Keeping your distance

At all times, you must make sure to stay a safe distance from the vehicle in front of you, and be satisfied that you can stop within the distance that you can see to be clear.

What is the advantage to a motorcyclist of staying well back from the vehicle in front while riding?

It gives the rider a safe braking distance.

In good weather, you should maintain at least a two-second gap from the vehicle in front, and more in poor conditions. This gap gives you sufficient room to brake safely in the event that the vehicle in front slows or changes direction suddenly. It also allows you to see the road in front of the vehicle ahead.

What should a motorcyclist be aware of when following close behind a larger vehicle?

They will be in the blind spot of the driver of the vehicle in front.

Their visibility to oncoming traffic will be reduced.

If you ride too close behind a large vehicle, the driver of that vehicle may not be aware that you are there. You will also be hidden from the view of oncoming traffic.

What should a motorcyclist do if they are following a vehicle on a wet road and an overtaking vehicle pulls into the gap between them and the vehicle in front?

Ease back to regain a safe distance.

When in traffic on a wet road, you should allow at least a four-second gap between you and the vehicle in front. If another vehicle overtakes you and pulls into this gap, you should slow down and restore the four-second gap between you and the vehicle in front.

Braking and stopping

While you are learning to ride, one of the most important skills you need to master is how to slow down, brake and bring your bike to a stop. Your bike has front and rear brakes and you need to learn how to use them individually and together.

When should the rear brake of a motorcycle be used on its own?

During slow manoeuvres.

Under normal circumstances, you should apply the front brake just before the rear brake. The front brake is considerably more powerful than the rear. However when travelling at very slow speeds, using the rear brake alone can result in smoother control.

When should a motorcyclist avoid using the front brake?

When the motorcycle is banked over, turning or on a loose surface.

What should a rider avoid doing when a motorcycle is banked over?

Using the front brake.

Avoid using the front brake while banked over in bends, while turning at a junction, and on loose surfaces. Using the front brake in these situations can cause the motorcycle to straighten up in the road and go straight on, or cause the loss of tyre grip, leading to a skid. If you must brake on a bend, use the rear brake.

What should a motorcyclist do when descending a long steep hill?

Engage a lower gear at an early stage.

When descending a long steep hill, you should use engine braking to maintain a steady speed. Changing down a gear or two increases the effect of the engine braking. This reduces wear on the brakes, and helps ensure that they do not overheat and that they are more effective when needed.

What should a motorcyclist do when descending a steep and winding road?

Use the brakes on the straight only.

It is always safer to brake when travelling upright in a straight line. On a steep and winding road, you should use a combination of engine braking and the normal brakes as necessary on approaching the bends. Braking in a bend can cause the bike to straighten up and go straight on, or to a loss of tyre grip leading to a skid.

When should a motorcyclist brake firmly?

Only when travelling in a straight line.
Only on the straight.

It is always safer to brake when travelling upright in a straight line. You should avoid braking on bends, and always adjust your braking to suit the road conditions.

How should a motorcyclist apply both brakes?

Apply the front brake followed by the rear.

How should braking force be distributed when stopping a motorcycle on a straight road in dry conditions?

Apply slightly more pressure to the front.

How should braking force be distributed when stopping a motorcycle on a straight road in wet or slippery conditions?

Apply the same amount of pressure to both brakes.

To stop safely in good weather and road conditions, you should apply the front brake followed by the rear. More pressure should be applied to the front, as this gives the best stopping power. In wet or slippery conditions, you should apply equal pressure to front and rear brakes

What has an effect on stopping distance?

The speed of the motorcycle.

Tyre condition.

Road conditions.

Reaction time.

You should always travel at a speed that will enable you to react and respond correctly and safely to a situation. Stopping distance is the sum of reaction distance and braking distance.

Reaction time is the time it takes to react to a change in traffic or road conditions. An alert and fit rider takes between half a second and one-and-a-quarter seconds to react. In this time, a motorcycle travelling at 80km/h will travel about 15 metres before the brakes are even applied. Reaction time can be negatively affected by age, alcohol, drugs, fatigue, state of health and mental condition.

Speed affects the stopping distance of a motorcycle. In dry conditions at 50km/h, stopping distance is typically 24 metres, whereas at 100km/h this increases to 78 metres.

Road surfaces that are wet, icy or loose reduce tyre grip, and extend your stopping distance considerably. At 80km/h on a good dry road, stopping distance is typically 53 metres, whereas on a wet road this increases to 81 metres.

Worn or improperly inflated tyres reduce the grip of your tyres on the road, with the result that your motorcycle may skid during an emergency stop.

What effect has a sidecar on the stopping distance of a motorcycle?

It increases stopping distance, especially going downhill.

The extra weight of the sidecar increases the stopping distance, especially going downhill.

What is the stopping distance of a vehicle travelling at 80km/h on a good dry road?

53 metres.

When travelling at 80km/h in good dry conditions, stopping distance is approximately 53 metres. This is made up of 15m reaction distance and 38 metres braking distance.

Stability and skidding

The most common cause of a skid is going too fast for the road conditions, or jerky braking, gear changing or steering. You can reduce the likelihood of skidding by riding smoothly at an appropriate speed, and by keeping your distance from the vehicle in front. Be particularly careful when approaching bends, especially those on a downslope. Don't rely on your ABS to prevent you from skidding – it won't always do so.

What might cause a rider to lose control of a motorcycle?

Water on the road.
Wet leaves on the road.
Mud on the road.

You are more likely to skid or lose control of your motorcycle in bad weather conditions, when road surfaces tend to be more slippery. You should be on the alert for wet surfaces, mud or gravel, and wet leaves on the road. These conditions will be more hazardous near bends or at junctions where you will need to brake, accelerate or change direction.

What effect could crossing tram tracks at an oblique angle have on a motorcycle?

It could destabilise the motorcycle.

You should cross train or tram tracks with caution, especially when they are at an oblique angle to your path. The road surface may be uneven. The tracks may not be at the same level as the road, and your motorcycle may lose stability while crossing the tracks.

What can happen if a rider applies both brakes, with greatest pressure on the rear?

The rear wheel may lock.

When you apply the brakes on the motorcycle, your weight and that of the motorcycle shift forward onto the front wheel, and the weight on the rear wheel is reduced. If you apply too much braking force to the rear wheel at this stage, it may lock up, causing a skid. Under normal conditions, you should apply the front brake first, followed by the rear, with the greater pressure on the front.

What should a motorcyclist do if the throttle sticks open while they are riding along?

Operate the engine cut-out switch.

In an emergency situation, such as the throttle sticking open, you should use the 'kill' switch (emergency engine stop) to stop the engine and bring the motorcycle safely to a halt. This switch may also be used to stop the engine after a collision or a fall.

What is a possible effect of riding over road markings such as lines and directional arrows?

Tyre grip may be reduced, particularly in wet weather.

The paint used in the road markings can be slippery, especially in wet weather. You should try to avoid riding over these markings where possible.

What in particular should a motorcyclist be aware of when crossing tram tracks?

The tracks may be slippery, particularly when wet.

You should approach tram and railway crossings with caution. The road markings and tracks can be slippery, especially in wet weather. You should also look out for broken road surfaces on these crossings.

What would be the result of excessive use of mirrors?

Ability to read the road ahead would be impaired.

You should read the road ahead and react accordingly. Using the mirrors excessively or looking behind excessively will distract your main focus from the road in front and may extend your reaction time.

What can a motorcyclist do to reduce the risk of skidding?

Accelerate gently.

Excessive acceleration can cause the front wheel of your motorcycle to lift from the road or cause the rear wheel to spin. Each of these causes a loss of stability and may lead to the motorcycle going out of control or skidding. Always use gentle acceleration and ride within your own limits.

What action can a motorcyclist take to avoid skidding?

Avoid using the front brake when the motorcycle is banked over.

As motorcycles have less tyre contact on the road than other vehicles, you should always brake in a controlled manner. Avoid using the front brake when the machine is banked over in order to reduce the risk of skidding.

What action should a motorcyclist take if the rear wheel skids under acceleration on wet surfaces?

Ease off the throttle.

Take care when accelerating in wet conditions. Too much acceleration can cause the rear wheel to skid, with the risk that you will lose control of the bike. If the rear wheel does start to skid, ease off the throttle to reduce the power going to the rear wheel.

Alert driving and consideration for other road users

You need to be fully alert when you are riding a motorcycle, so don't ride when you are very tired. Tiredness is a factor in many road collisions.

You should also behave with consideration and courtesy towards other road users, including pedestrians, cyclists, motorists and drivers of larger vehicles.

How other drivers see you

As a motorcycle rider, you must constantly bear in mind that you are not as visible to other road users as, for example, cars, trucks or buses. You must try to make sure that you avoid situations that put your own life or that of other road users in danger.

What in particular should a motorcyclist be aware of when approaching a junction from which a vehicle is emerging?

The driver of the emerging vehicle may underestimate the motorcyclist's speed.

What in particular should a motorcyclist be aware of when approaching a side road?

Drivers of emerging vehicles may not see the motorcyclist.

As a motorcyclist, you are a vulnerable road user. You should pay particular attention when approaching side roads as the drivers of emerging vehicles may not have seen you. If in doubt slow down and try to make eye contact with the driver. You should always ride defensively and be prepared to stop if necessary.

What in particular should a motorcyclist be aware of when travelling on a dual carriageway?

Other vehicles may change lane without checking their blind spots.

When you are travelling on a dual carriageway, you should read the road ahead and be prepared for the possibility that other traffic may change lane without making proper observations or giving adequate warning.

What in particular should a motorcyclist be aware of when following a large truck or bus?

Vehicles emerging from side roads may not see the motorcycle behind the larger vehicle.

When you are on a motorcycle following behind a large truck or bus, you will not be easily visible to motorists emerging from side roads. Always read the road ahead and allow plenty of space between your motorcycle and the vehicle in front.

In general, how can a motorcyclist make other road users more aware of their presence on the road?

Avoid travelling in other vehicles' blind spots.

By riding in a position where they can be seen and keeping a good distance from other traffic.

You should always try to make other road users aware of your presence on the road. Where possible, avoid travelling in other road users' blind spots and ride in a position in which you can be seen by other drivers. Avoid riding too close to the vehicle in front.

See and be seen

High hedges and the winding nature of country roads can impair visibility – blind corners, sharp bends and dips in the road can be particularly dangerous. You should always adjust your speed to suit the road you are driving on and you must never exceed the speed limit. In many cases, a safe speed might be much less than the stated speed limit for the road. You need to be able to stop the bike in the road space that you can see – if you can't, you're going too fast.

You should also make sure that other road users can see you.

What should a motorcyclist do to improve their ability to see in very heavy rain?

Reduce speed.

In heavy rain, reduce speed. This gives you more time to see and react to changes in road and traffic conditions.

What should a motorcyclist do to improve their visibility to other road users?

Wear reflective or fluorescent material.

Drive with a dipped headlight on.

> Motorcyclists are less visible to other road users, so they need to increase their visibility by wearing bright or reflective clothing and by riding with their dipped headlight on.

Under what circumstances should a motorcyclist take a 'life saver' look?

Before making a U-turn.

Before changing lane.

Before changing direction.

> A 'life saver' look is a look over the left or right shoulder to observe the blind spot area which is not covered by the mirrors. This should be done before you move off, before you change your position on the road and before you make a U-turn.

What should a motorcyclist do before making a U-turn?

Take a 'life saver' look and check the road is clear in both directions.

> Before making a U-turn a motorcyclist should always take the appropriate observations to the rear, including a 'life saver' look. A 'life saver' look is a look over the left or right shoulder to observe the blind spot area which is not covered by the mirrors.

When riding a motorcycle around a bend on an unlit road at night with no oncoming traffic, which light should a motorcyclist use?

Full beam headlight.

> On an unlit road at night, you should use your main beam headlight to help you see and be seen. However, use dipped headlights when there is approaching traffic or pedestrians on the road.

Under what circumstances should a motorcyclist use full high-beam headlights?

When riding on unlit roads at night.

Use full high-beam headlight when riding on unlit roads at night. When you have the full beam light on, a blue warning light is shown on the instrument panel.

What should a motorcyclist do when travelling on a main road with traffic emerging from side roads who may not see the motorcycle?

Look well ahead and read the road.

When you are travelling along a road that has many junctions with emerging traffic, try to read the road ahead and be prepared to react and respond to any vehicle turning into your path. Always adjust your speed to suit the road and traffic conditions.

When riding on a main road, a motorcyclist sees a vehicle emerging from a side road into their path. What action should the rider take?

Slow down and be ready to stop.

Try to read the road ahead and be prepared to react and respond to any vehicle turning into your path. Be ready to slow down or stop if necessary.

How can riding a more powerful motorcycle change the rider's attitude?

The motorcyclist may have the impression that they are travelling slower than they actually are.

Powerful motorbikes tend to be quiet, produce little vibration and go fast without straining the engine. On such a bike, you might gain speed without realising it and find yourself in a situation that you cannot control.

What should a motorcyclist do before changing lanes from left to right?

Check mirrors, indicate and give 'life saver' look to the right.

You should check your mirrors, indicate and give a 'life saver' look to the right to make sure that it is safe to change lane.

Bad roads, bad weather and bad times of day

As a motorcyclist, you are particularly vulnerable on uneven road surfaces, in bad weather and in poor lighting conditions. You must learn to deal with these hazards by adjusting your style of driving, and particularly by lowering your speed so that you can react safely and in good time to any changes in road or traffic conditions.

What lights must be shown by a motorcyclist at night?

Headlight, red rear light, number-plate light and red rear reflector.

On a moped or motorcycle, you are legally required to have a headlight, a red rear light, a number plate light and a red rear reflector. These should be checked regularly and kept clean. This will help to ensure that you can be seen at night.

What lights should a motorcycle show when parked at night on an unlit road?

A white light to the front and a red light to the rear.

If a motorcycle is parked on an unlit road at night, it creates a potential danger for other road users. It is the rider's responsibility to ensure that their motorcycle can be seen, so they must switch on their vehicle's parking lights (white to the front and red to the rear). On most motorcycles, this can be done by turning the key another click past the 'lock' position on the ignition switch, after which the key can be removed.

How can strong winds affect a motorcyclist?

They can blow the motorcyclist off course.

A sudden gust of wind can blow a motorcyclist off course, especially in cross winds. Take extra care in windy conditions, as there is a danger that you will be blown into the path of other vehicles.

What should a motorcyclist do when travelling in fog?

Slow down, use dipped headlight and keep to the centre of the driving lane.

When travelling in fog, use your dipped headlight and maintain a position in the centre of your lane. Drive with extreme caution and be prepared to react and respond to changes in road or traffic conditions.

What in particular should a motorcyclist be aware of when travelling in hot weather and the tar on the road is melting and soft?

The road may be slippery.
Stopping distances are increased.

In very hot weather, tarmac road surfaces can become soft. When this happens, you should take extra care when braking and cornering, as tyre grip will be reduced.

Bright sunlight can make it difficult for other road users to see what?

The indicators on a motorcycle.

In bright sunlight, a motorcycle's brake lights and indicators might not be clearly seen. In such circumstances, you should consider giving a clear hand signal to inform other road users of your intentions.

Scope of the motorcycle driving licences and learner permits

The questions in this section deal with what is allowed and what is not allowed by the various categories of motorcycle driving licence and learner permit.

Under what circumstances may the holder of a motorcycle learner permit carry a pillion passenger?

Never.

It is against the law for the holder of a motorcycle learner permit to carry a pillion passenger at any time.

What is the maximum engine capacity of the motorcycle that the holder of a category A1 driving licence may ride?

125cc.

The holder of a category A1 driving licence is restricted to riding motorcycles of 125cc or less, with a power rating of 11kw or less.

What is the maximum engine capacity of the motorcycle that the holder of a category M driving licence may ride?

50cc.

The holder of a category M driving licence is limited to riding a moped of 50cc or less, that is designed to go no faster than 45km/h.

A category M driving licence restricts the holder to riding motorcycles with what maximum design speed?

45km/h.

The holder of a full category M licence is limited to riding motorcycles that are designed to go no faster than 45km/h.

Is the holder of a category A, A1 or M learner permit or full driving licence permitted to drive a quadricycle?

No.

A category A, A1 or M learner permit or licence does not permit the holder to drive a four wheel quadricycle under any circumstances.

If a motorcyclist wishes to ride a motorcycle with an engine power output of more than 11 kilowatts, which category of licence must they hold?

Category A.

If you wish to ride a motorcycle with engine power greater than 11 kilowatts, you must have a category A licence.

What is the maximum engine power of a motorcycle that may be ridden by a person holding a full category A licence for less than 2 years?

25 kilowatts.

For how many years is the holder of a full category A licence restricted to riding motorcycles with a engine power of 25 kilowatts or less?

2 years.

When the holder of a category A restricted learner permit passes their driving test, the licence restriction is carried over to the full licence for the first two years. During this time they are limited to riding motorcycles with a power rating of 25kw or less.

What is the maximum engine power of a motorcycle that may be ridden by a person holding a category A1 licence?

11 kilowatts.

A category A1 driving licence limits the holder to riding motorcycles with a maximum engine power output of 11 kilowatts.

What is the minimum engine capacity that a motorcycle must have in order to travel on a motorway?

50cc.

To travel on a motorway, a motorcycle must have an engine capacity of 50cc or more and be capable of travelling at least 50km/h.

Other drivers and passengers

The questions in this section deal mainly with carrying pillion passengers legally and safely.

Under what circumstances may a child be allowed to ride a motorcycle in a public place?

Never.

> The minimum age at which a motorcycle can be ridden in a public place is 16. A motorcycle learner permit cannot be issued to anyone under this age.

How should a motorcyclist maintain their balance while carrying a passenger on the motorcycle?

Instruct the passenger to lean over on bends in the same direction as the rider.

> In order to maintain proper balance and control of your motorcycle when carrying a passenger, you should advise the passenger to lean the same way as you do when travelling around bends.

Under what circumstances is a passenger allowed to sit sideways on a motorcycle?

Never.

> Passengers should always sit on a motorcycle facing forward with both feet on the footrests.

Environmental impact of motorcycling

The motor industry is making substantial efforts to reduce the environmental damage caused by driving. Modern cars and motorcycles are generally much more efficient in their use of fuel, have lower greenhouse gas emissions, and cause less pollution.

As individual motorcyclists, we can also do quite a lot to reduce our personal carbon footprint and to minimise the impact our road use has on the environment.

What would be the effect of taking the exhaust off a motorcycle?

Noise and smoke pollution would increase.

The exhaust is fitted to an engine to control noise and smoke pollution. If it is removed, noise and smoke pollution is increased. The performance of the engine is also affected.

Getting off the motorcycle

In general, you should get off the bike on the left side – this means that you will be on the side away from other traffic. When dismounting, pay attention to the difference in level between the road and the kerb, and be careful of slippery underfoot surfaces – such as loose gravel.

What should a motorcyclist do before getting off a motorcycle?

Look behind to make sure it is safe.

You should always look behind before getting off a motorcycle. In general, you should get off on the left-hand side, away from traffic.

What should a motorcyclist do before a passenger gets off the motorcycle?

Look behind to make sure it is safe.

You should always look behind before allowing a passenger to get off your motorcycle. The passenger should get off on the left-hand side, away from traffic.

Part 4

Trucks and buses

Necessary documents

The questions in this section deal with the restrictions imposed by different categories of bus and truck licence and the regulations regarding roadworthiness testing.

How frequently must a vehicle be submitted for certificate of roadworthiness test?

Annually.

All commercial vehicles – that is, goods vehicles, buses carrying more than 8 passengers, and ambulances – must be tested for roadworthiness (commercial vehicle test or CVT) when they are one year old and annually after that.

What learner permit drivers in categories C, C1, D and D1 are required to be accompanied by the holder of a full licence?

All.

If you hold a learner permit for category C, C1, D or D1, you must be accompanied and supervised at all times while driving by someone who holds a current full driving licence for the same category of vehicle.

What is the maximum Design Gross Vehicle Weight of a trailer that a driver can tow on a full category D Licence?

750kg.

The maximum Design Gross Vehicle Weight of a trailer that can be towed on a full category C or D licence is 750kg. If you need to tow a trailer with a Design GVW greater that 750kg, you must hold an EC or ED licence.

Driving hours and rest periods

EU regulations on driving hours were introduced to reduce the incidence of driver fatigue, which is a known risk factor in road collisions. If you drive a bus or truck, there are detailed regulations relating to the hours you may drive, and the breaks and rest periods you must take. The purpose of these rules is both to improve your working conditions and to contribute to road safety by reducing the risk of your becoming fatigued. The questions in this section are designed to check that you know and understand these regulations.

What is the maximum permitted number of hours that a driver can drive without taking a break?

4.5 hours.

You are required to take a rest period after 4.5 hours driving.

What is the maximum number of hours that a driver can drive in a given week?

56 hours.

EU regulations specify that a driver can drive no more than 56 hours in a given week.

What is the maximum permitted number of driving hours in a two-week period?

90 hours.

EU regulations specify that a driver can drive no more than 90 hours in a two-week period.

What is the minimum break time that should be taken for each break during or following a driving period?

15 minutes.

EU regulations specify that a driver must take a break of at least 15 minutes during or following a driving period.

What is the minimum break time which must be taken following a 4.5 hour driving period?

45 minutes.

EU regulations specify that a driver must take a break of at least 45 minutes after driving for 4.5 hours.

What is the maximum number of hours a driver may drive in week two, if 56 hours were worked in week one?

34 hours.

EU regulations specify that a driver can drive no more than 90 hours in a two-week period.

On how many days of the working week may a driver drive for more than 9 hours?

2.

EU regulations specify that a driver must not drive for more than 56 hours a week, with a maximum of 10 hours a day for two days, 9 hours a day for four days and at least one full rest day.

On how many days of the working week may a driver drive?

6.

EU regulations specify that a driver must not drive on more than six days in any week and must not exceed 56 driving hours in the week.

On three days of the week what can the minimum daily rest period be reduced to?

9 hours.

EU regulations specify that a driver must take an 11-hour rest period within each 24-hour period. This may be reduced to 9 hours on a maximum of three days in a two-week period.

What is the normal minimum weekly rest period?

45 consecutive hours.

EU regulations specify that a driver must normally take two rest periods, each of 45 consecutive hours, in a two-week period.

On a rest day, may a driver carry out other 'paid duties' apart from driving?

No. It is a rest day.

EU regulations specify that a driver is not permitted to do any paid work on a rest day, driving or otherwise.

What does this tachograph symbol mean?

Driving period.

What does this tachograph symbol mean?

Period when the driver is available to work.

What does this tachograph symbol mean?

Other work – that is, work other than actual driving.

What does this tachograph symbol mean?

Rest period.

Tachographs (recording devices) are required to be fitted to trucks over 3.5 tonnes and to buses with more than 9 seats. They record the driver's driving activity, rest periods, vehicle speed, distance travelled and other information.

The driver should select the symbol that represents the activity they are engaged in – for example, rest, driving or other work. The records must be retained for inspection by Enforcement Officers.

What tachograph rules apply to a cross-border or international journey?

EU rules continue to apply irrespective of the vehicle's location.

All EU Member States apply uniform regulations with regard to tachographs.

Who is responsible for ensuring that a tachograph chart is properly completed and inserted into the tachograph?

The driver.

When must a new tachograph chart be placed in a tachograph?

At the start of each working day.

Who is responsible for making sure that a driver's card is properly inserted into the digital tachograph unit?

The driver of the vehicle.

EU regulations require the driver to keep daily records.

In a vehicle with an analogue tachograph, the driver is responsible for ensuring that the tachograph chart is properly completed and inserted into the tachograph at the start of each working day. In a vehicle with a digital tachograph, the driver is required to insert their driver smart card into the digital tachograph unit when taking charge of a vehicle.

What information is recorded on a tachograph chart?

Driving time, vehicle speed and distance.

Breaks and rest periods.

The tachograph chart records a driver's driving hours, vehicle speed, and distance covered. It is used to check that the driver takes at least the legal minimum amount of rest during the working day.

Which tachograph records must be retained by the driver?

Records for the current day and the 28 calendar days immediately preceding that day.

EU regulations require the driver to keep records for the current and the previous 28 days, and to produce them on demand.

What time and day denote the beginning of a week for tachograph purposes?

00.00 hours on Monday.

The tachograph chart records a driver's driving hours, vehicle speed, and distance covered. It is used to check that the driver takes at least the legal minimum amount of rest and does not exceed the legal maximum driving hours in a day, week or fortnight. For tachograph purposes, the week starts at 00.00 hours on Monday and finishes at 24.00 hours on Sunday.

If a driver drives two or more vehicles as part of a working day, what are the tachograph requirements?

Use the same tachograph chart or card in each vehicle.

EU regulations require that, if driving more than one vehicle in a day, a driver must use the same tachograph chart in each vehicle. If the chart from the first vehicle is not compatible with the equipment fitted to the second vehicle, a new chart should be used. You must keep your digital tachograph card with you at all times while driving.

If two drivers are intending to use the same vehicle in a given day what should the first driver do?

Remove their tachograph chart when they leave the vehicle and insert it again when they recommence driving the vehicle.

If, in a given day, two drivers intend to use the same vehicle fitted with a digital tachograph, what should the first driver do?

Remove their driver's card from the digital tachograph unit of the vehicle when they leave it.

EU regulations specify that if a vehicle is being driven by more than one driver in a given day, each driver must use their own driver's card in slot one of the digital tachograph unit while they are operating the vehicle and remove it when leaving the vehicle. If the vehicle has an analogue tachograph, each driver should use their own tachograph chart for that day.

Why is it important to comply with break period requirements?

Without regular breaks, the driver could become tired while driving.

EU regulations specify that a driver must take a break of at least 45 minutes after driving for 4.5 hours. During this break, the driver is not allowed to drive or undertake any other work.

Under what circumstances can a driver's rest period be taken in a parked vehicle?

If the vehicle is fitted with a bunk.

Drivers are required to take a daily rest period of at least 11 hours. This can be broken down into one uninterrupted period of 3 hours and a second uninterrupted period of at least 9 hours. Drivers may take their rest periods in a parked vehicle only if the vehicle is fitted with a bunk.

What can a bus or truck driver do to stay alert on a long journey?

Wind down the window and reduce the temperature in the driver's compartment.

Fatigue is a known risk factor in road collisions.

EU regulations specify legal minimums for rest periods so that drivers are able to drive their vehicles in a safe manner. During a journey, a driver should take planned rest breaks, avoid making the driving area too warm, and avoid eating large, heavy meals.

What in particular should a professional driver who works long hours be aware of?

Fatigue affects alertness and ability to react.

Professional drivers must avail of regular adequate rest periods to avoid fatigue. EU regulations on driving hours specify legal minimum rest periods, and maximum driving hours in a day, week and fortnight.

What information is recorded on a driver's card?

Driving time, vehicle speed and distance covered.

Driver smart cards were introduced to prevent driving hours offences. The cards record driving hours, breaks and rest periods, vehicle speed, and distance travelled, as well as the driver's personal details, such as name, driving licence number, and photograph.

What driver records must be produced by a driver to an enforcement officer at a roadside inspection?

The driver's card.

Any analogue charts relating to the driver's use of vehicles fitted with analogue recording equipment in the preceding 28 calendar days.

Driving hours, rest periods and breaks are recorded by a tachograph, either digitally on the driver card or graphically on a tachograph chart. Drivers are legally required to carry records of activity for the preceding 28 days and to produce these records for inspection when requested by enforcement officers.

A driver is required to drive two or more vehicles fitted with digital tachographs at different times during their working day. One of the vehicles is used during a period which is exempt and 'out of scope' from driver's hours and tachograph requirements. What should the driver do?

Use the tachograph's manual input facility to record 'other work'.

Where a driver performs both 'in-scope' and 'out of scope' (exempt driving) in the same week, the out-of-scope driving can be recorded by manual entry on the digital tachograph unit.

A driver is working away from a vehicle and the driver's card is not inserted in the digital tachograph. What should the driver do?

Manually enter times and activities in the tachograph.

Driver smart cards were introduced to prevent driving hours offences. If at the start of the working day a driver is engaged in non-driving duties away from the vehicle, they should manually enter a record of the other work activities into the digital tachograph when they take the vehicle in charge.

Journey planning

As a professional bus or truck driver, your job will involve transporting passengers or goods safely and efficiently from one location to another. The better you plan your routes, the less stressful your journey will be, and you can also achieve greater fuel efficiency. The consequences of not planning journeys adequately can be much more serious for drivers of large vehicles than for drivers of smaller vehicles – for example, in a truck you do not want to find yourself having to reverse out of a narrow street that you turned into in error or because you did not have clear route directions.

What factors could influence the driver's choice of route?

Humpback bridges.

> When planning a route, a driver needs to take the height, width, length and weight of the vehicle into account. These characteristics help the driver to determine which routes can be safely negotiated in the vehicle and which ones are unsuitable. For example, a route with a humpback bridge might not be suitable for a large vehicle.

When estimating the time for a journey, what should a driver allow extra time for?

Driving during 'rush-hour' traffic.

Stoppages due to road works.

Driving during adverse weather conditions.

Mandatory rest breaks.

Minor repairs to the vehicle.

Delays due to traffic incidents.

> A journey will nearly always take longer than expected because of traffic jams, road works, adverse weather conditions, and so on. A driver should understand this and allow sufficient time to complete the journey in a safe manner.

A driver comes to a bridge with a weight limit that is lower than their vehicle's weight. What should the driver do?

Turn around and find an alternative route.

> A driver should know the weight of their vehicle, and if they encounter a regulatory sign indicating a weight limit that is lower than their vehicle's weight, they must not proceed past the sign. They should take an alternative route.

Vehicle weights and dimensions

Trucks and buses can vary considerably in length, height and weight.

When you are driving a bus or a truck, you need to develop an understanding and awareness of where you are on the road in relation to other vehicles, to street furniture (such as bollards and lamp posts) and to other objects – including road signs, overhanging trees, traffic islands and so on. Coming to terms with the size of the particular vehicle you are driving is essential.

You also need to know details about the weight of your vehicle, and the weight bearing on each axle. EU and national rules govern the maximum weights of different kinds of truck and bus, and you are responsible for ensuring that your vehicle is in compliance.

What does the maximum permitted weight of the vehicle refer to?

The weight of the vehicle plus the weight of the load which may be carried.

The maximum permitted weight refers to the gross vehicle weight – this is the sum of the empty weight plus the maximum weight the vehicle is allowed to carry.

What does 'design gross vehicle weight' mean?

Vehicle weight plus the maximum load weight which the vehicle is designed to carry.

The design gross vehicle weight is the weight of the vehicle plus the weight of the heaviest load that may be carried in it, as specified by the manufacturer.

What is the maximum permitted rear load overhang that does not require a red flag or marker?

1 metre.

What is the maximum permitted rear load overhang with a red flag?

3 metres.

When is a red flag a sufficient marker for a rear-load overhang that exceeds one metre?

Only during the day.

In order to warn other road users, loads extending from the rear of a vehicle by more than 1 metre must be clearly marked with a red flag or marker by day and by a lamp by night. The overhang must not exceed 3 metres.

What is the maximum permitted side-load overhang in millimetres?

305mm.

The maximum side-load overhang normally permitted is 305 millimetres (1 foot). To carry a load with a greater overhang, you need an abnormal load permit, which can be obtained from An Garda Síochána.

What is the maximum permitted length of an articulated vehicle?

16.5 metres.

The maximum permitted length of an articulated vehicle is 16.5 metres. To drive a longer vehicle or load, you must apply for permits from the Local Authorities of the areas through which you will be driving and/or An Garda Síochána.

Braking systems

Most buses and trucks have three different brakes: the standard foot brake and the parking brake that you are familiar with from driving a car and a retarder / exhaust brake. You must know how and when to use them to control the speed of your vehicle and to stop it safely and effectively.

What does a speed limiter do?

Prevents the vehicle from exceeding a pre-set speed.

A speed limiter is a device fitted to HGVs and buses which sets the maximum speed at which the vehicle can travel.

What does an engine governor do?

Prevents the engine from over revving.

An engine governor is a device fitted to the engine's fuel pump. It limits or controls the amount of fuel delivered to the engine, and prevents the engine from over-revving.

Given similar road conditions and vehicle speeds, what braking distances will a truck or bus/minibus need compared to a car?

Longer distances.

When driving a car on a good road in good weather, the driver should leave at least a 2-second gap between them and the vehicle in front. A larger vehicle needs a bigger gap, because of its greater weight and momentum. The driver should allow at least a 4-second gap under normal conditions, and even more on wet or icy roads.

How can a driver reduce speed without using the footbrake?

By lifting their foot off the accelerator.
By engaging the retarder, if fitted.

If a driver reads the road ahead and reacts early enough, they can generally (unless going downhill) reduce speed simply by taking their foot off the accelerator. This style of driving prolongs the life of the vehicle's brakes, reduces fuel consumption and emissions, and improves passenger comfort.

Endurance braking systems (or retarders) are standard equipment on many trucks and buses. They enable the driver to reduce speed without using the wheel-mounted brake (or service brake). Retarders are particularly useful when descending hills, as they help to extend the life of the brakes and to prevent brake fade.

On a vehicle equipped with an air-brake system, what is the first indication of low air-pressure?

A warning light comes on and /or a buzzer sounds in the cab.

Most modern HGVs and buses are fitted with air brakes. If air pressure drops in the braking system, a warning light and/or buzzer alerts the driver. If this happens, you should pull in and stop safely before total loss of air pressure.

After moderate use of the brakes, a driver notices that the air-gauges are not returning to normal. What should the driver do?

Stop safely and build up air pressure.

If the air-brake gauges are reading low, what could this indicate?

There is an air-leak in the braking system.

Most modern HGVs and buses are fitted with air brakes. If, after moderate use of the brakes, the air pressure gauges do not return to normal, the driver should stop in a safe place and try to build up air pressure. If the gauges remain low, the driver should suspect an air leak, and not drive the vehicle until it is rectified. Driving with an air leak can cause the brakes to lock on and immobilise the vehicle, which could cause an obstruction or a hazard to other traffic.

Technical matters, with a bearing on road safety

Buses and trucks have a number of safety features that are not generally found on cars. You should be familiar with the systems on the vehicle you are driving. You should also carry out routine checks on your vehicle before undertaking any journey.

If a driver notices that a wheel nut is missing what should be done to balance the wheel?

Have the nut replaced before driving.

The driver should check the condition of the wheel nuts as part of the daily inspection of the vehicle. If any wheel nuts are missing, the driver should have them replaced before commencing a journey. The nuts should be tightened to the manufacturer's recommended torque, and checked and if necessary retightened after travelling a short distance.

What does this symbol mean?

Electrical cut-off switch.

For safety reasons, buses and some trucks are fitted with an electrical cut-off switch. This enables you to disconnect battery power from all the vehicle's systems. It is especially important to use this switch in the event of an incident where there is a fire or fuel spill.

What does a load-sensing valve do?

Adjusts the brake pressure which is applied at the wheels.

A load-sensing valve regulates the pressure passing to the brakes, so that maximum pressure is available only when the vehicle is fully laden. As the load on the vehicle reduces, the valve automatically lowers the braking pressure.

What does 'road-friendly' suspension do?

Reduces the impact of a vehicle's weight on the road.

Road-friendly suspension, also known as air suspension, protects the load in a vehicle by reducing vibration. It can also reduce the damage to road surfaces and bridges caused by heavy loads.

What would be the likely effect of a defect in the power steering system?

It could make the steering seem heavy and stiff to turn.

What would indicate to the driver that there was a problem with the power steering?

Inability to easily turn the steering wheel.

Power steering is a system that reduces the effort that a driver needs to turn the front wheels. It generally consists of a fluid reservoir and a hydraulic pump powered by the engine. If the pump malfunctions or the fluid level drops, steering the vehicle may become very difficult.

A bus or truck is in regular use. How often should it be completely visually inspected?

Daily.

A driver must carry out a complete visual check on their vehicle, both internally and externally, every day. These checks increase safety, reduce operating and maintenance costs, help avoid breakdowns and result in better customer service.

Why is it dangerous to drive when the vehicle is not in gear?

It eliminates engine braking when steering or slowing.

Driving a vehicle when the engine is not engaged (that is, when the gears are in neutral or the clutch is depressed) is known as coasting.

You should avoid coasting, as it reduces your control of the vehicle and your ability to brake.

What is the purpose of a diff-lock?

It locks up the differential to improve traction on soft ground.

When should a driver use a diff-lock on a truck?

When stuck on soft ground.
When stuck on snow or ice.

The diff-lock has been engaged to enable a truck to move off on a slippery road surface. When should the driver disengage it?

As soon as the truck is underway.

A driving axle is fitted with a differential, which allows the wheels on either side to rotate at different speeds, so that the vehicle can negotiate bends and corners.

The purpose of a diff-lock is to cause the wheels to rotate at the same speed, and this is used when extra traction is required, for example if the vehicle is stuck in mud or snow. The diff-lock should be used only at low speed and should be disengaged as soon as possible.

What effect can wet weather have on the vehicle's exterior mirrors?

It can distort the rear vision of the driver.

When you are driving in the rain, water droplets can adhere to the exterior mirrors and obscure your view to the side and rear of the vehicle. If your vehicle has heated mirrors, turn them on to clear them. Alternatively, stop periodically to clear them manually.

What should a driver's mirrors reflect?

As much as possible of the road that is not in the driver's direct line of vision.

In a large vehicle, the driver's view all round the vehicle is severely restricted. The driver should make sure to properly adjust and keep clean all external and blind-spot mirrors, and to check them before carrying out manoeuvres such as moving off, changing lane, or reversing.

Why should spray suppression equipment be fitted to a large vehicle?

To reduce the amount of water sprayed up from the wheels.

When a vehicle is driven on a wet road, its wheels throw up spray, and this has the potential to reduce visibility for other drivers. A spray suppression system generally includes mudguards, rain flaps and wheel skirts designed to reduce the amount of spray generated by a vehicle. A driver should check the spray suppression equipment on the vehicle before setting out on a journey, especially in bad weather.

What is the function of the transmission system in a truck or bus?

To transmit power from the engine to the wheels.

The transmission system of the engine is made up of the clutch, gearbox and driveshafts. Torque power is transmitted from the driveshaft of the engine to the road wheels via the clutch and gearbox to make the vehicle move.

Air turbulence

Large vehicles, such as trucks and buses, create considerable air turbulence, particularly when travelling at speed. This can affect the stability of other road users, particularly pedestrians, cyclists and motorcyclists, and put them off their course. Large vehicles can also throw up large quantities of water, dust and debris from the road surface, and this can prevent other road users from seeing properly and controlling their vehicles. The questions in this section check that you understand these issues.

Who might be badly affected by the air-turbulence caused by a passing high-sided vehicle?

Pedestrians.

Cars towing caravans.

Motorcyclists.

Cyclists.

> A high-sided vehicle creates air turbulence to the sides and rear of the vehicle, and this turbulence increases with the speed of the vehicle. This affects other road users, and in particular pedestrians, cyclists, motorcyclists and cars towing caravans. The driver should take extra care when passing such road users, to avoid blowing them off course.

What is the effect of a large vehicle's slipstream on a motorcyclist it is overtaking?

The motorcyclist can be blown off course.

What is the effect of a large vehicle's slipstream on a cyclist it is overtaking?

It can affect the cyclist's stability.

> A high-sided vehicle creates air turbulence to the sides and rear of the vehicle, and this turbulence increases with the speed of the vehicle. The driver should take extra care when passing cyclists or motorcyclists.

What can happen if a vehicle displaces dust or debris from the road?

The dust and debris can discomfort pedestrians or cyclists and make it difficult for them to see where they are going.

> Dust and debris displaced from the road by a large vehicle can make it difficult for other road users to see. This is both uncomfortable and unsafe.

What in particular should the driver of a large vehicle be aware of when passing pedestrians?

The pedestrians can be affected by the vehicle's slipstream.

The driver of a large vehicle should always show due care and consideration for vulnerable road users such as pedestrians. This is particularly important in rural areas where there are no footpaths, and in bad weather. Spray, dust or debris thrown up from the wheels can make it difficult for the pedestrian to see, and the air turbulence created by the vehicle can blow them off course.

Weather-related matters

Rain, snow, ice, fog and high winds all present challenges for road users, and particularly for drivers of large vehicles, such as trucks and buses. You should make sure that you are well prepared for bad weather, and that you know how to adopt an appropriate style of driving for the conditions. The questions in this section deal with driving in bad weather.

What should a driver do before starting a journey in bad weather?

Check the weather forecast for the road and weather conditions.

Top up the windscreen washer reservoir.

Driving in bad weather is more dangerous and more tiring. You should check the weather forecast and other sources for information on the expected conditions on the intended route, and allow extra time to complete the journey.

Before starting any journey, you are legally required to make sure that the vehicle's windscreen wipers are working and that the vehicle has sufficient windscreen washer fluid. These checks are particularly important if bad weather is expected.

What should a driver ensure when driving a diesel engined vehicle in cold weather?

That winter-grade fuel is used.

In extremely cold weather, diesel fuel is liable to freeze, particularly in the fuel lines. To prevent this, in winter you should use diesel fuel that has had an anti-waxing agent added to it.

How should a descent be negotiated in snow or frosty weather?

Engage a lower gear and use gentle braking applications to keep the speed down.

In snow or ice, a vehicle takes longer to stop. Before starting a descent in a large vehicle in such conditions, reduce speed and select a lower gear. Brake gently and only when needed. If the vehicle is fitted with a manually selectable retarder, engage it before starting the descent.

When driving in heavy rain, what should a driver do?

Drive at a slower speed to allow for reduced visibility and increased braking distance.

Switch the windscreen wipers on to high and drive at a reduced speed.

When driving in the rain, your visibility can be severely reduced both by the rain itself and by the spray thrown up by other road users. Stopping distances on wet roads are greater than on dry, and you should reduce speed accordingly.

What should a driver do when overtaking a vehicle which is displacing mud and spray?

Use the vehicle windscreen wipers and washer system.

What should a driver do when overtaking a large vehicle that is throwing up spray?

Move out earlier than normal and give extra clearance.

In wet weather, vehicles tend to throw up spray and mud, and this can affect visibility for other road users. To minimize this danger, read the road ahead, and when overtaking move out earlier than usual, giving the vehicle you are overtaking extra clearance. This will reduce the amount of spray being deposited on your windscreen.

Before starting a journey make sure that the windscreen wipers are working and the washer reservoir is topped up. Then use these systems as necessary to clear the windscreen, especially when overtaking other vehicles.

Driving large or high-sided vehicles

Driving a large or high-sided vehicle presents particular challenges for the driver. You need to be familiar with the vehicle you are driving, so that you can manoeuvre and control it in all road, traffic and weather conditions. If you are driving a particular vehicle for the first time, you should familiarise yourself with its features and controls before taking to the road. And you should always be aware of the effect that your vehicle has on other road users.

What effect can strong winds have on a high-sided vehicle?

They can increase the likelihood of the vehicle overturning.

The winds can reduce the vehicle's stability.

When driving a high-sided vehicle in strong winds, what should a driver avoid?

Suspension bridges.

When driving a high-sided vehicle in strong winds, the driver should choose a route that avoids high-level roads and bridges, exposed motorways and dual carriageways.

What would help to stabilise a high-sided vehicle in windy conditions?

Having a full load.

A high-sided vehicle being driven in strong winds is more stable if it has a full, evenly distributed load.

Why is a large vehicle likely to intimidate other road users?

The size and noise of the vehicle.

Other road users can be intimidated by the sheer size and noise of a large vehicle, but the driver should never deliberately frighten other road users, for example by revving the engine, by driving too close to them or by repeatedly pressing the footbrake to create loud hissing noises.

When someone is driving a vehicle that is different to the vehicle they normally drive or with which they are unfamiliar, what should they do?

Drive initially with extra care and at a lower speed than normal.

When someone is driving a vehicle that has features with which the driver is unfamiliar, what in particular should the driver be aware of?

The height, weight, length and width and/or the controls may differ from the vehicle usually driven by the driver.

If you are required to drive a vehicle that is different to the vehicle you normally drive or with which you are unfamiliar, you should take time to familiarise yourself with the controls and operating systems. You should also learn the height, length, width and weight of the vehicle, so that you can comply with any restrictions you meet on the road.

When driving the vehicle initially you should take extra care and drive at lower speeds than usual until you become accustomed to the vehicle.

When driving a large vehicle, why is it sometimes necessary to move to the right before making a left-hand turn?

To ensure the nearside rear wheels clear the corner.

A driver is driving a long vehicle and wishes to turn left into a narrow side road. What should the driver do?

Move to the right on the approach to allow the turn be made without mounting the kerb.

Be aware that cyclists may come up on the inside if the vehicle has moved to the right to make room to turn left.

If you are driving a long vehicle and wish to turn left into a narrow road, take as much room as you need on the approach to the junction to allow you to complete the turn successfully. This may mean that your vehicle will be to the right of its normal position on the road, and other road users, especially cyclists, may come up on the inside of your vehicle.

When driving a large vehicle on a road which has overhanging trees, what should a driver do?

Drive in the normal position but move out as necessary to avoid hitting overhanging branches.

When driving a large vehicle on a road that has overhanging trees, maintain your normal position on the road as far as possible, but move out as necessary to avoid hitting the trees, and return to the normal position as soon as you can.

When driving a low-loader vehicle, what should a driver allow for?

Narrow bridges.

Humpback bridges.

Overhead cables.

A low loader is a semi-trailer used to transport heavy oversized vehicles. When loaded, it may be higher, wider and lower than a standard vehicle. If you are driving such a vehicle, you should be aware of these extra hazards and plan your route accordingly, avoiding, where necessary, obstacles such as humpback or narrow bridges and overhead cables.

When driving an articulated car-transporter, what should a driver be aware of?

The front overhang follows a wider line than the cab.

When driving a car-transporter, what should a driver plan ahead for?

Low bridges.

Overhanging trees.

Overhead cables.

The driver of a car transporter should be aware of the extra height of the vehicle when it is loaded with the cars, the instability of the vehicle when only the top deck is loaded, and, on articulated car transporters, the fact that front overhang does not follow the line of the cab when turning.

When driving a large vehicle around a roundabout, what precaution should the driver take to avoid roll-over?

Reduce speed.

A vehicle can become unstable and roll over if it changes direction sharply while being driven too fast. For this reason, when driving a large vehicle, you should slow down on approaching a roundabout to reduce the likelihood of rolling over.

What in particular should a driver be aware of when driving a low-bodied vehicle over a steep humpback bridge?

Ground clearance.

When driving a vehicle with a low body, you should take care that the vehicle is not 'grounded'. You need to make sure that you have sufficient ground clearance when, for example, going over railway level crossings or humpback bridges.

What particular characteristics of the vehicle should a driver consider when planning a route?

The length, width, weight and height of the vehicle.

When planning a route, you need to take the height, width, length and weight of your vehicle into account. These characteristics help you to determine which routes can be safely negotiated in the vehicle and which ones are unsuitable. You should avoid getting into a situation where you need to turn or reverse.

When entering a loading bay or refuelling depot, what should a driver be aware of?

The height, width and length of the vehicle.

Before entering a loading bay or refuelling depot with a large vehicle, you should make certain, based on your knowledge of the vehicle's dimensions, that it can be manoeuvred safely into and out of the space available. You should make sure that you avoid hazards such as overhanging canopies, building support pillars, fuel pumps, staff and pedestrians.

What should a driver be aware of when driving a vehicle that has a high centre of gravity?

The vehicle is more likely to roll over on a bend or roundabout.

If you are driving a large vehicle with a high centre of gravity, you should slow down on bends, corners and roundabouts. The vehicle can become unstable and roll over if it changes direction sharply while being driven too fast.

A driver is driving a large vehicle up a steep hill. There is a 'slow lane' on the left. What should the driver do?

Drive in the slow lane.

Slow lanes (also known as crawler or climbing lanes) have been introduced on some roads to allow large slow-moving vehicles get out of the way of faster-moving traffic. When driving a large vehicle, you should use such lanes where possible to help improve traffic flow.

The driver of a large vehicle needs to proceed straight ahead at a mini roundabout at which there is limited space to manoeuvre. What should the driver do?

To the extent possible, negotiate the mini roundabout in the same way as a normal roundabout.

Mini-roundabouts generally function as traffic calming measures. They do not always provide sufficient room for a large vehicle to negotiate them in the same way as a normal roundabout. The driver must evaluate the situation on approach and respond in a way that is appropriate for the size of their vehicle, while yielding as appropriate to other traffic.

What should the driver of a large vehicle be aware of when being overtaken by a motorcyclist in windy weather?

The wind turbulence will make the motorcycle less stable.

When a motorcyclist is overtaking a high-sided vehicle, the turbulence created by the larger vehicle may affect the motorcyclist's stability.

After overtaking another large vehicle, what should a driver do before moving back into the left-hand lane?

Check the left-hand mirror, signal, and move back when it is safe to do so.

Before overtaking a large vehicle on a dual carriageway or motorway, you should check your right-hand mirror, signal and move out into the right-hand lane when it is safe to do so.

After overtaking the vehicle, check your left-hand mirror, signal and move back in to the left-hand lane when it is safe to do so. Do not cut too quickly across the vehicle you have just passed.

What should the driver of a large vehicle consider before overtaking another large vehicle?

The speed of the vehicle being overtaken.

The speed of oncoming traffic.

The width and length of the driver's own vehicle.

The width and length of the vehicle being overtaken.

The width and condition of the road.

The weight and load distribution of the driver's own vehicle.

Before overtaking another large vehicle, you need to assess the road ahead, and take into consideration the speed of the vehicle you are driving and the size and speed of the vehicle you intend overtaking. You should be sure that you can complete the manoeuvre safely. Overtaking a large vehicle with a large vehicle takes more time and greater distance than a similar manoeuvre involving two cars.

Always make sure that you can complete the overtaking manoeuvre safely.

You should know the total weight and the weight on each axle of your vehicle, and you should also be aware of roads with vehicle weight and axle restrictions.

When driving a truck or a bus in traffic on a dual carriageway, what should a driver do?

Allow sufficient stopping distance from the vehicle in front.

Always keep a safe distance between your own vehicle and the vehicle in front in case the vehicle in front stops suddenly. Drivers of large vehicles should never drive in close convoy, even when travelling with other vehicles from the same company.

Restricted vision

When you are driving a bus or truck you must be able to see the traffic and road conditions ahead, and, as far as possible, also be able to check to the sides and rear of your vehicle. This means making sure that your seated position is good, that the windows are clean and in good condition, and that your mirrors are clean and properly adjusted.

How can sunlight affect visibility in a vehicle with grimy windows?

It can create a mirror effect and reduce visibility.

> When driving in sunny weather all the vehicle's windows should be clean. A grimy or greasy windscreen can impair your ability to see the road ahead and compromise your ability to react and respond to changing conditions.

When driving a large vehicle, what is the most effective way for the driver to ensure that they can see to the side and rear of the vehicle?

Making full use of exterior mirrors.

> When driving a large vehicle you should make full use of your exterior mirrors so that you are constantly aware of what is happening around you, and that you can react and respond appropriately.

How can the height of the cab affect the driver's ability to see other road users?

A high cab can make it more difficult to see pedestrians and cyclists adjacent to the cab.

> In a high cab it can be more difficult to see pedestrians and cyclists that are adjacent to the cab. They may be out of sight below the windscreen line and/or side window line. Blind-spot mirrors should be fitted and should be used particularly when moving off and in slow-moving traffic.

What should a driver do when the exterior mirrors are covered with a film of dirt or grime?

Stop the vehicle and clean the mirrors before continuing.

> A driver should always ensure that they can see clearly in their exterior mirrors. If you discover that your mirrors are dusty or dirty, you should clean them before continuing so that you have maximum visibility of the road around you.

Safety of loads and passengers

When you are driving a bus or truck, it is your responsibility to make sure that the vehicle is not overloaded, and that your vehicle does not pose a danger to other road users.

When stopping for a short period of time in an urban area, for example to let off passengers or unload goods, what should a driver do?

Avoid causing an obstruction to other road users by parking close to the left.

When stopping or parking to deliver goods or collect passengers, you should stop in a location that does not cause obstruction to other road users.

How can overloading affect a vehicle?

The vehicle's stability can be affected.

The effects of overloading a goods vehicle include damage to the road surfaces, damage to the vehicle itself, and loss of stability in the vehicle, possibly leading to a serious incident. Overloading is against the law, punishable by fines and imprisonment.

Getting out of a vehicle

When letting passengers out of your vehicle, or when getting out yourself, you should make sure that you are doing so safely, and that you are not putting other road users in danger.

What precaution should a driver take to secure the vehicle before getting out of it?

Check that the handbrake is on and the ignition is switched off.

Before you leave your vehicle, apply the handbrake and switch off the ignition. Check to make sure that you can open the door safely without endangering others, and alight when it is safe to do so. Remember to secure the vehicle by closing windows and locking all doors.

What precaution should a driver take when allowing passengers to alight from a bus or minibus?

Make sure that the passengers exit on the side away from the centre of the road.

Before allowing passengers off the bus, you should stop close to the kerb on the left to allow passengers an easy and safe exit from the vehicle.

Driving in tunnels

If you are driving a large vehicle through a tunnel, your driving behaviour can present a hazard to yourself and to other road users. The questions in this section check that you understand how to drive in tunnels and how to respond to situations that might arise in a tunnel.

Before driving through a tunnel, what should a driver do?

Check that the height of the vehicle is less than the signed limit.

Check the tunnel height before starting the journey.

Take off sunglasses to improve vision.

If your route takes you through a tunnel, you must make sure in advance that your vehicle does not exceed the height limit for the tunnel. If your vehicle is higher than the limit displayed on the tunnel height-limit sign, you must take an alternative route.

Be aware that there is considerably less light available in a tunnel, even with the tunnel lights on. If you are wearing sunglasses, remove them before entering the tunnel.

When driving through a tunnel, what should a driver do?

Maintain a safe distance from the vehicle in front.

When entering a tunnel in a large vehicle, slow down and allow a 100-metre gap between your vehicle and the vehicle in front. Because of its size, your vehicle might make it more difficult for following traffic to see the road ahead.

If there is unexpected traffic congestion in a tunnel, what should a driver do?

Switch on hazard warning lights.

If, when driving a large vehicle through a tunnel, you meet traffic congestion, leave a safe distance between you and the vehicle in front and switch on your hazard warning lights when stationary.

If a driver comes to a halt in stationary traffic in a tunnel, what should they do?

Switch off the engine.

If, when driving a large vehicle through a tunnel, you are halted in stationary traffic for any length of time, you should switch off the engine to reduce fumes in the tunnel and conserve fuel.

If a vehicle being driven through a tunnel breaks down, what should the driver do?

Switch on the hazard warning lights.

Call for help from an emergency station.

Use the emergency telephone to call for help.

If, when driving a large vehicle through a tunnel, your vehicle breaks down or is involved in an incident, switch on the hazard warning lights, switch off the engine, and use the emergency phone at the emergency station to call for help.

If a vehicle being driven through a tunnel goes on fire, what should the driver do?

Leave the vehicle immediately and use the emergency phone at the nearest emergency station.

If, when driving a large vehicle through a tunnel, a fire breaks out in your vehicle, switch off the engine, leave the vehicle immediately, use the emergency phone at the emergency station to alert the tunnel operator, and leave the tunnel at the nearest available exit.

Taking emergency/corrective action

A truck or bus that is not equipped with anti-lock brakes (ABS) goes into a front-wheel skid. What should the driver do?

Pump the footbrake.

> If you are driving a truck or bus that is not equipped with ABS and a front-wheel skid develops, pump the footbrake rapidly. This is known as 'cadence braking' and it can prevent or stop a vehicle from skidding.

Collisions

As the driver of a bus or truck, you must know how to act if you are involved in a collision or other traffic incident.

How should following traffic be warned in the event of an incident?

By placing a red warning triangle on the road a short distance back from the vehicle involved.

Under what circumstances should a driver use an emergency red warning triangle?

In the event of an incident or breakdown.

> If your vehicle breaks down, or is involved in an incident, place a red warning triangle on the road, far enough from the incident to give following traffic adequate warning.

Environmental matters

The motor industry is making substantial efforts to reduce the environmental impact of driving. Modern vehicles are generally much more efficient in their use of fuel, have lower greenhouse gas emissions, and are less polluting than older vehicles.

As individual drivers, we can also do quite a lot to reduce our personal carbon footprint and to minimise the impact our driving has on the environment. The questions in this section test your knowledge of environment-friendly driving.

What should a driver do to avoid excessive exhaust pollution from their vehicle?

Have the vehicle serviced regularly.

How could a driver reduce exhaust pollution?

Make sure that the engine is serviced regularly.

You can reduce the amount of exhaust pollution created by your vehicle by reducing speed, avoiding severe braking and harsh acceleration, and having the vehicle serviced regularly.

How would a driver improve efficiency?

Use gentle acceleration and make gear changes to maximize efficiency.

To improve fuel efficiency, save money and help the environment, you should reduce speed, brake and accelerate gently, and change gears efficiently, as recommended by the vehicle manufacturer.

Other matters

There are a few situations that present unique challenges for bus and truck drivers. These include night driving, motorway driving, using the 'slow lane' and dealing with vulnerable road users. The questions in this section check that you understand the issues involved and know how to respond.

When driving a truck at night, how should a driver keep alert?

Keep plenty of cool air circulating in the cab.

Take rest periods, preferably walking in fresh air.

> Stay alert by keeping the cab of the vehicle cool and by taking the required rest periods. A break, including a walk in fresh air and/or a caffeine drink can also be beneficial.

When joining a motorway from a slip road, what should a driver do?

Adjust speed to match that of the motorway traffic, and merge into a suitable gap.

> When joining a motorway from a slip road, adjust your speed to that of the motorway traffic and merge into a suitable gap. This may mean slowing to allow traffic in the nearside lane to pass. You should not force them to swerve or slow down to avoid your vehicle.

A large vehicle is being driven up a steep hill and there is a 'slow lane' on the left. What should the driver do?

Drive in the slow lane to allow other traffic overtake.

> Slow lanes (also known as crawler or climbing lanes) have been introduced on some roads to allow large slow-moving vehicles get out of the way of faster-moving traffic. When driving a large vehicle, you should use such lanes where possible to help improve traffic flow.

What road users are most vulnerable at junctions?

Pedestrians.

Motorcyclists.

Cyclists.

> When emerging from a junction, you should watch out for other road users such as pedestrians, who often cross at junctions. Cyclists and motorcyclists are often difficult to see at junctions and may approach faster than you think.

When a driver meets a set of traffic lights showing green and elderly pedestrians are crossing at the junction, what should the driver do?

Allow the pedestrians to cross in their own time.

A driver meets a pelican crossing with a green light showing. There is a pedestrian still on the road. What should the driver do?

Wait patiently and let the pedestrian cross at their own pace.

If you are driving and meet a pelican crossing or a set of traffic lights that are showing green in your favour, but with pedestrians on the crossing, you should allow the pedestrians to cross in their own time. Vehicles do not have an automatic right of way on the road and should proceed with caution at all times.

What road users should the driver of a large vehicle be particularly aware of on their left-hand side at traffic lights?

Pedestrians.

Motorcyclists.

Cyclists.

When at traffic lights in a large vehicle, you should watch out for vulnerable road users, such as pedestrians, cyclists and motorcyclists, who may come up on your left. Before moving off, check along the left to make sure it is safe to proceed.

Part 5
Trucks only

Driving licences and learner permits

The questions in this section test that you know what the holder of each category of driving licence and learner permit is allowed and not allowed to do.

What category of licence must a driver hold in order to drive a vehicle with a maximum design gross vehicle weight of 7,500kgs with seating for no more than 8 passengers?

C1 or C.

What is the maximum design gross vehicle weight that the holder of a category C1 licence may drive?

7,500kgs.

To drive a rigid vehicle with a design gross vehicle weight of between 3,500kg and 7,500kg, you must hold a category C1 licence. Above 7,500kg DGVW, you need a category C licence.

What category full licence must a driver hold before applying for a category EC (articulated truck) learner permit?

C.

What category full licence must a driver hold before applying for a category EC1 (light truck and trailer) learner permit?

C1.

Before you apply for a learner permit for a vehicle towing a trailer, you must hold a full driving licence for the towing vehicle. So, for example, you must hold a B licence before applying for an EB learner permit, and you must hold a C1 licence before applying for an EC1 learner permit.

Is the holder of a category C1 full licence entitled to tow a trailer?

Yes, up to 750kgs gross vehicle weight.

If you hold a full category C1 licence, you may tow a trailer with a design gross vehicle weight of 750kg or less. However, if you hold a category C1 learner permit, you may not tow a trailer.

What is the minimum age a driver must be in order to obtain a category EC (articulated truck) driving licence?

What is the minimum age a driver must be in order to obtain a category EC1 (light truck and trailer) driving licence?

18 years.

The minimum ages for the different categories of licence are as follows:

Licence category	Minimum age
A1, M, W	16 years
B, EB	17 years
A, C1, C, EC1, EC	18 years
D1, D, ED1, ED	21 years.

Is the holder of a category C learner permit entitled to tow a trailer when driving a category C vehicle?

No, the holder of a category C learner permit may not tow a trailer.

Is the holder of a category C full driving licence entitled to tow a trailer when driving a category C vehicle?

Yes, provided the trailer does not exceed 750kgs gross vehicle weight.

If you hold a learner permit for category B, C1, C, D1 or D, you may not tow a trailer.

A full licence holder in one of these categories may tow a trailer with a design gross vehicle weight of 750kg or less.

What is the maximum number of passengers that can be carried by the holder of a category C or C1 licence?

8 passengers.

If you hold a category C or C1 licence, you are permitted to drive vehicles with seating for up to 8 passengers plus the driver.

What does the plated weight of a vehicle refer to?

The maximum gross laden weight at which it is allowed to be driven.

Goods vehicles normally have a plate fitted showing the maximum gross weight, the maximum axle weights, and the train weight. These maximum weights must be complied with when the vehicle is used on the road.

What does this information sign indicate when displayed on a truck or trailer?

The type of material carried.

This sign indicates the type of material carried and the level of hazard associated with it.

Vehicle weights

There are a number of regulations relating to the weight of the vehicle. There are different requirements depending on the weight of the vehicle, the number of axles and the type of suspension. As a truck driver, you are expected to know and comply with these requirements.

What must an articulated truck weighing 44 tonnes GVW have?

Anti-lock brakes, air suspension and 6 axles.

An articulated truck with a GVW of 44 tonnes is required to have six axles, anti-lock brakes and air suspension.

What is the maximum permitted laden weight in tonnes of an EC (articulated truck) on 6 axles with a conventional suspension (non air)?

40 tonnes.

What is the maximum laden weight in tonnes of a 4-axle rigid truck with conventional (non air) suspension?

30 tonnes.

What is the maximum permitted laden weight in tonnes of a 4-axle rigid truck with road friendly (air) suspension?

32 tonnes.

What is the maximum permitted laden weight in tonnes of a 3-axle rigid truck with conventional (non air) suspension?

25 tonnes.

What is the maximum permitted laden weight in tonnes of a 2-axle rigid truck with conventional suspension?

18 tonnes.

Overloading any truck is illegal and can have serious consequences. The maximum permitted laden weight of different types of truck is set out in the following table.

Type of truck	Maximum permitted laden weight
6-axle articulated truck with conventional suspension	40 tonnes
4-axle rigid truck with conventional suspension	30 tonnes
4-axle rigid truck with road-friendly suspension	32 tonnes
3-axle rigid truck with conventional suspension	25 tonnes
2-axle rigid truck with conventional suspension	18 tonnes

Speed limits

The general speed limit that applies to trucks is lower than the general speed limit for cars. If you are driving a truck, you must know and respect this limit. As with all speed limits, it is a maximum permitted speed – not a target speed.

What is the maximum permitted speed of a truck?

80km/h.

What is the maximum permitted speed of a truck on a motorway?

80km/h.

> Goods vehicles with a design gross vehicle weight of more than 3,500kg are limited to a maximum speed of 80km/h on all roads including motorways. However you should always adjust your speed to suit road and traffic conditions, and comply with posted speed limits.

Braking and speed limiters

Certain trucks are required to have a speed limiter installed, and certain trailers are required to have a braking system. The questions in this section test your knowledge of these issues.

What is the maximum speed limiter setting on a category C vehicle?

90km/h.

What is the design gross vehicle weight above which trucks must be fitted with a speed limiter?

3,500kg.

> Goods vehicles with a design gross vehicle weight of more than 3,500kg must be fitted with speed limiters that restrict them to a maximum speed of 90km/h. The general speed limit for such vehicles, however, is 80km/h. You should always adjust your speed to suit road and traffic conditions, and comply with posted speed limits.

Does a trailer exceeding 750kgs (GVW) require a braking system to be fitted?

Yes.

A trailer must be fitted with brakes if it has a design gross vehicle weight of more than 750kg or it is more than half the laden weight of the drawing vehicle.

What might be the cause of a truck being unable to move off when the brake park lever is released?

Insufficient brake air pressure.

In the event of total loss of air pressure on a full air-brake system, the brakes can lock. If this happens, the brakes can be released only when air pressure is restored.

Technical matters with a bearing on road safety

Modern trucks have a number of features that contribute to their safety. As the driver, you should know how to use them, how to maintain them in working order, and how to recognise when they need to be repaired or serviced.

What does a warning buzzer in the cab indicate usually?

Low air pressure in the braking system.

Vehicles fitted with air brakes are equipped with a buzzer to alert the driver to a loss of air pressure. You should not attempt to drive while this buzzer is sounding. If the buzzer comes on when you are driving, pull over in a safe place as soon as possible. If your vehicle loses all air pressure, the brakes may lock on, which may cause an obstruction or hazard to other traffic.

What should be done with the air-lines of an uncoupled tractor unit?

They should be properly stowed away.

When uncoupling a tractor unit from a trailer, the air-lines should be stowed safely, using the hooks or other facilities provided for the purpose on the tractor unit. If you don't do this, the lines can get damaged, for example by getting burned by the exhaust system or getting tangled up in the drive shaft.

Why should the fifth wheel drawing plate on an articulated truck be sufficiently greased?

To reduce wear.

In order to prevent premature wear on the drawing plate and latching mechanism, the fifth wheel should be cleaned, inspected for damage and re-greased regularly. Keeping the fifth wheel well greased makes it easier to couple and uncouple a trailer, and also allows smoother articulation between the tractor and trailer when turning.

What should a driver check after driving a truck over rough or broken ground?

That stones are not jammed between the rear twin wheels

After driving a truck over rough ground, make sure that it has not picked up any rocks or debris between the rear twin wheels. You should also check this as part of your daily routine.

What is the purpose of a 'range-change' gearbox?

It offers the driver a selection of high and low gears to suit the load being carried or the terrain.

A 'range-change' gearbox offers a wider range of gears than a standard gearbox. By offering the choice of high or low ratios, it effectively doubles the number of gears available, so that the driver can choose the most appropriate gear for the road and the load being carried.

What is the advantage of a two-speed axle?

It doubles the number of gear ratios available to a driver

A two-speed axle doubles the number of gear ratios available to the driver by offering a choice of two final drive ratios in the rear axle. The selection is made by operating an electrical switch.

What does an unloader valve do?

It releases excess air pressure in the braking system.

An unloader valve prevents the build-up of excess pressure in the air tanks of a vehicle fitted with air brakes. The valve is fitted between the compressor and the air tanks. It opens and closes at pre-set pressures, and you will hear a change in the sound of the compressor as it operates.

Safety of vehicle loading

Vehicle manufacturers specify the maximum load that can be safely carried in the vehicle, and how that load should be distributed across the axles. As a truck driver, you need to know these specifications. You are responsible for making sure that your truck is not overloaded, that the load is properly positioned on the vehicle, and that it is secured in such a way that it will not pose a danger to people or property.

What additional precautions should be taken when transporting bulk liquid?

The tanks should be sectioned off.

Where possible, vehicles that carry bulk liquids should have the tank divided up into sections or have baffle plates installed to reduce the wave effect and help the driver to slow or stop the vehicle smoothly.

In relation to load distribution, what is the most important thing that must be taken into account?

That individual axle weights are not exceeded.

In relation to load distribution, what must be taken into account?

That the gross vehicle weight is not exceeded.

The Weights and Dimensions Plate specifies a vehicle's or a trailer's maximum permitted laden weight (also known as the design gross vehicle weight) and the maximum permitted laden weight on each axle.

It is illegal to carry a load that would cause the approved gross vehicle weight to be exceeded, as to do so would compromise the safety and stability of the vehicle.

What must be taken into account when part of the load has been removed?

That none of the axles have become overloaded because of transfer of weight.
That the remaining load is evenly distributed.

You must make sure that all loads are safely and securely loaded, and that the load is evenly distributed over the axles. You may have to redistribute the load after your initial deliveries to ensure continued stability.

What should a driver ensure with regard to the load they are carrying?

That it does not cause danger or nuisance to other road users.
That it does not cause the front axle weight to exceed the rear axle weight.

How might an unevenly distributed load affect a truck?

The truck's stability is adversely affected.

You must make sure that your load is safely and securely loaded, and that the load is evenly distributed over the axles.

An insecure or unbalanced load, or one that is too heavy, can compromise the safety and stability of the vehicle.

Make sure also that the load does not pose any danger or inconvenience to other road users.

What effect does sharp braking have on a loosely secured load?

The load tends to go to the front of the vehicle.

You must make sure that your load is safely and securely loaded. If you brake or change direction suddenly, an insecure load can shift or fall off, causing the vehicle to lose stability and creating a hazard for other road users.

What effect does increasing the load have on the vehicle's braking ability?

It increases the normal stopping distance required.

In general, a heavier load makes a truck more difficult to stop and increases the required stopping distance.

How does air suspension affect a vehicle's carrying capacity compared to that of a vehicle with conventional suspension?

It allows extra weight to be carried.

Air suspension (road-friendly suspension) provides the vehicle with an even load height, whether it is empty or fully laden. It allows for extra weight to be carried by the vehicle, and helps to protect fragile goods in transit.

How should a load of loose dusty material be carried?

It should be covered with a tarpaulin or sheeting.

Why should the cargo area of a truck carrying loose sand be covered?

To prevent the sand from blowing away.

When dusty material, such as sand or grain, is carried, the load should be covered with a tarpaulin or sheeting to avoid the load being lost by blowing off the vehicle and creating a hazard or nuisance for other road users.

What should a driver ensure when carrying hazardous materials?

That they comply with the regulations on the conveyance of dangerous substances by road.

If you are driving a vehicle that is carrying hazardous materials, you are responsible for taking all the appropriate precautions to ensure public safety.

The driver must be qualified to transport the specific material and the vehicle must be equipped with the relevant safety equipment and labels.

What should a driver ensure when carrying out an inspection under a raised tipper body?

That the body is supported by props.

Never carry out an inspection under a raised tipper body unless the body is properly supported by props. The prop used should be strong enough to hold the structure in place if the hydraulic raising system malfunctions.

What should a driver of a tipper truck be aware of when tipping a load from their vehicle?

Overhead cables and power lines.

Before raising the tipper body, check to see that there are no overhead cables or power lines that could be touched by the raised body. Failure to make this check could prove fatal.

When may the maximum weight which an axle is designed to carry be exceeded?

It may never be exceeded.

The maximum design weight of each axle and the maximum weight it is allowed to carry in Ireland (which may be less) must be displayed on a plate attached to the vehicle.

How is a lifting axle used?

It may be raised or lowered depending on the load being carried.

Rigid lorries, tractor units and trailers are often fitted with lifting axles. These axles may be free running or steered. The advantage of a lifting axle is that it can be raised or lowered to suit the load on the vehicle, thereby saving fuel and tyre wear.

What effect may the liquid load have on an articulated tanker when it is braking to a stop on a straight road?

It may push the vehicle forward.

What should a driver do when coming to a stop while driving a half loaded tanker which is not divided into compartments?

Ease off the footbrake.

When braking in a tanker carrying a liquid load (particularly one that is partially loaded), you should be aware of the 'wave effect' caused by the motion of the fluid in the tank. This may cause the vehicle to surge forward when you ease pressure on the brakes. For this reason you should ease off the brake gently.

In what circumstances is an articulated truck more likely to jack-knife?

When it is unloaded.

If, while driving an articulated truck, you brake sharply or slow down quickly, the trailer may pivot around the tow hitch coupling and cause both vehicles to go off course, and possibly overturn. This is more likely to occur on an unladen vehicle, where there is less weight on the driving axle.

Why is it important to distribute the weight evenly between the axles when loading a heavy goods vehicle?

To ensure maximum stability.

To ensure the stability of your vehicle, you must make sure that the load is evenly distributed between the axles. In addition, the load should be secured against the headboard to prevent it from moving forward under braking, and heavy items should be placed at the bottom to prevent the vehicle from becoming top-heavy.

Who can be held responsible if a truck is found to be overloaded?

Both the driver and the owner.

Both the owner and the driver can be held responsible if a goods vehicle is found to be overloaded on a public road.

Who is responsible for making sure that a truck's load is secure during a journey?

The driver.

It is the driver's responsibility to know how a vehicle has been loaded and how the load has been secured. You should also check your load at regular intervals, as it may settle or move during the journey, thereby causing the straps or chains to loosen.

What are twist locks used to secure?

A steel cargo container onto a vehicle or trailer.

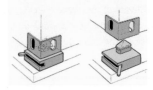

How should an ISO cargo container be secured to a vehicle?

With twist locks.

Lift on/Lift off ISO containers should be carried only on skeletal trailers or flat bed trailers equipped with proper twist locks. You must ensure that these twist locks are in the unlocked position when the container is being lifted on or off the trailer, and that they are locked into the container while in transit.

What action should a driver take if they are required to make an urgent delivery of a container and notice that some of the twist locks or container securing devices are broken?

They should not drive until the twist-locks have been repaired or replaced.

The driver is responsible for the security of their load. If the twist locks are defective on a container-carrying vehicle, the container could fall off the vehicle on a bend or roundabout, causing damage to property and creating a hazard for other road users.

How should a load of steel scaffolding poles be secured?

Secured firmly with strong chains or similar devices.

Steel scaffolding poles should be loaded against the headboard of the trailer and secured with strong chains or similar devices. You should stop at regular intervals during the journey to check the tension of the chains or straps.

How should steel girders be loaded on a vehicle?

In such a way that the weight is evenly distributed on the vehicle.

What should a driver ensure when their load consists of steel girders?

That the girders are properly secured with strong chains or similar devices.

Steel girders should be loaded against the headboard of the vehicle or trailer, and their weight distributed evenly between the axles to ensure stability. They should be secured with strong chains or similar devices. If web straps are used, the webbing should be protected where it passes over the corners of the girders.

You should stop at regular intervals during the journey to check the tension of the chains or straps.

Why are ropes unsuitable to tie down a load of girders?

Because they may wear and snap.

Sharp edges on the girders can cause the ropes to fray and snap, with the result that your load becomes insecure. If a load has sharp edges, you should use web straps with suitable sleeves to protect the webbing from the sharp edges.

What effect will momentum have on a vehicle carrying a load of steel girders when it is turning a corner?

It will push the vehicle away from the bend.

The momentum of a heavily laden vehicle tends to push it straight on while cornering. This effect is more pronounced at higher speeds and with heavier loads.

You should bear this in mind when approaching bends, and adjust your speed accordingly.

What should a driver do if their load of steel girders comes loose during a journey?

Stop in a safe place and have the load re-secured.

You should check the security of your load at regular intervals during a journey. If a load of steel girders comes loose, stop in a safe place and secure the load. Do not continue the journey until the problem is rectified.

What is the most important thing for a driver to check before reversing into this loading bay?

For the presence of other people.

When reversing in haulage and distribution yards, you must watch out for people getting in and out of adjacent vehicles and pedestrians who may walk behind the vehicle.

What should a driver ensure before using a tail lift?

That the ground is level.

What should a driver ensure before operating a tail lift?

That there are no pedestrians or vehicles present.

Before using a tail lift, make sure that the vehicle is parked on level ground. Failure to do this can result in a loaded pallet rolling off the tail lift or toppling to the ground, causing damage or injury to pedestrians in the area.

Make sure that there are no pedestrians, vehicles or other obstacles in the area adjacent to the tail lift.

When driving a truck with hazardous goods or substances, who is responsible for ensuring that a hazchem sign is displayed?

The driver.

If you are driving a truck carrying hazardous goods, you must ensure that the correct symbol or mark is clearly displayed on the vehicle. In the event of a collision, the information provided by the sign provides vital information for the emergency services.

What is the maximum permitted distance between a drawing vehicle and a trailer?

4.5 metres.

The maximum permitted distance between a drawing vehicle and a trailer is 4.5 metres. A larger distance between the vehicles might lead other road users to believe that the two vehicles were independent and they might try to enter the space between them.

A warning device or flag must be attached to a drawbar when it exceeds what length?

1.5 metres.

The maximum permitted distance between a drawing vehicle and a trailer is 4.5 metres. Where it exceeds 1.5 metres, a warning device, such as a white flag of at least 30 centimetres, must be attached, to draw attention to the tow bar.

Vehicle safety equipment

When you are driving a truck, you must ensure that your vehicle does not present a hazard for other road users. You are required to have reflector stripes on the back of the vehicle, and under-run barriers to help prevent serious injury in the case of a collision.

What colour rear markings must be fitted to a category C type vehicle?

Red reflector stripes.

All category C type vehicles must have reflective markings on the sides and rear. The markings on the rear of the vehicle must be red; those on the sides can be white or amber.

What is the purpose of rear under-run barriers?

To prevent cars from going under the body of the vehicle from the rear.

Rear under-run barriers are protection barriers attached to the rear of a truck, trailer or semi-trailer. They are designed to prevent small vehicles such as cars and light vans from going under the truck if it stops or decelerates suddenly, and thus help to avoid or reduce serious or fatal injury.

Getting into, out of and onto the vehicle

In most trucks, the driver's seat is considerably higher than in a car. Getting into and out of the cab involves climbing up or down, and it is important that you do so safely. Before you get out, check that opening the door will not interfere with other road users, and that you can get down safely.

If you drive a tanker, take care when mounting the tank that you do not endanger yourself or others.

How should a driver get out of a truck cab?

Use the step and handrails provided while facing towards the cab.

> To safely exit the cab of a truck, first check whether it is safe to do so, and then climb down facing towards the cab, using the handrails for support.

What should a driver take into account when mounting a tanker?

That there may be overhead cables.

What should a driver be aware of when mounting a tanker?

That the tank might be slippery.

> If you need to mount the tank of your vehicle, check that the tank is not slippery and that the vehicle is not parked beneath overhead cables. Either of these conditions can cause injury or fatality.

Caring for the environment

Because of their weight and size, the loads that they carry, and the locations they operate in, trucks can cause particular problems for the environment, some of which can create hazardous conditions for other road users. Drivers of tipper trucks and trucks carrying loose loads need to be especially aware of these issues.

When driving a tipper truck and about to exit a quarry, what should a driver ensure?

That the tailboard is secured.

That there are no stones lodged between the twin-wheels.

That the wheels and mudguards are not covered with mud or other debris.

When driving a HGV, you must make sure that the vehicle is roadworthy and that it will not cause a hazard to other road users. Before leaving a quarry, check that the vehicle and its load will not compromise road safety. Make sure that mud or debris will not be spread on the road from the wheels or underbody, and that the tailgate has been securely shut. Also make sure that rear lights and reflectors are clean.

Motorway driving

In what circumstances may a truck driver use the hard shoulder of a motorway?

When stopping in an emergency or breakdown.

If, when driving on a motorway, your vehicle develops a problem, leave the motorway immediately if possible. If this is not possible, pull in and stop on the hard shoulder as far as possible to the left. Turn on your hazard lights and contact the emergency services without delay.

Bus lanes

A truck driver is late with a delivery and there is a bus lane in operation ahead, what should a driver do?

Not drive in the bus lane.

Bus lanes are operational at the times indicated on the accompanying plate. Only buses, taxis and cyclists may drive in the bus lanes at these times.

Part 6

Buses only

Driving licences and learner permits

The questions in this section test that you know what the holder of each category of driving licence and learner permit is allowed and not allowed to do.

What full licence category must a driver hold in order to obtain a category ED (large coach and trailer) learner permit?

D.

Before you can apply for a learner permit in category ED (large coach and trailer), you must hold a full D licence.

What full licence category must a driver hold in order to obtain a category ED1 (minibus and trailer) learner permit?

D or D1.

Before you can apply for a learner permit in category ED1 (minibus and trailer) you must hold a full D or D1 licence.

Is the holder of a category D or D1 learner permit allowed to carry passengers for hire or reward while driving a bus?

No.

The holder of a learner permit driving a car, van, bus or coach must not carry any passengers for payment of any kind.

Must the holder of a category D learner permit who holds a category D1 full licence display L-plates on a bus or coach while taking driving lessons?

Yes, at all times.

The holder of a learner permit (in every category except A1, A and M) must always display proper L-plates on the front and rear of the vehicle they are driving.

Must the holder of a category D learner permit who already holds a category D1 full licence be accompanied by the holder of a category D licence when driving a bus or coach?

Yes, at all times.

A learner permit holder in category D must always be accompanied and supervised by the holder of a full licence in that category.

Is a driver who holds a full category D licence restricted to automatic transmission (code 78) permitted to drive a conventional manual bus or coach on that licence?

No.

If you pass your driving test in a vehicle equipped with automatic transmission, a code 78 is noted in the restrictions column of your full licence. This restricts you to driving only vehicles with automatic transmission. If you subsequently wish to drive a manual vehicle in that category, you must obtain a new learner permit and comply with the regulations pertaining to learner permits, including L-plates and accompanying driver.

Who is required to hold a road passenger transport operator's licence?

A person or firm with a business involved in transporting persons by road for reward.

In order to operate a business involved in the transport of persons for reward by road, the operator must hold a road passenger transport operator's licence. For the full period of validity of the licence, the operator must employ a transport manager who holds a certificate of professional competence in road passenger transport.

Speed limits

The general speed limit that applies to buses is lower than the general speed limit for cars. If you are driving a bus, you must know and comply with this limit. As with all speed limits, it is a maximum permitted speed – not a target speed.

What is the maximum permitted speed on a **motorway** of a **single-decker** bus or minibus (having passenger accommodation for more than 8 persons) and which **is not** designed to carry standing passengers?

100km/h.

What is the maximum permitted speed on a **dual carriageway** of a **single-decker** bus or minibus (having passenger accommodation for more than 8 persons) and which **is not** designed to carry standing passengers?

100km/h.

What is the maximum permitted speed on a **national primary road** of a **single-decker** bus or minibus (having passenger accommodation for more than 8 persons) and which **is not** designed to carry standing passenger?

80km/h.

What is the maximum permitted speed on a **motorway** of a **double-decker** bus or minibus (having passenger accommodation for more than 8 persons) and which **is not** designed to carry standing passengers?

100km/h.

What is the maximum permitted speed on a **dual carriageway** of a **double-decker** bus or minibus (having passenger accommodation for more than 8 persons) and which **is not** designed to carry standing passengers?

100km/h.

What is the maximum permitted speed on a **national primary road** of a **double-decker** bus or minibus (having passenger accommodation for more than 8 persons) and which **is not** designed to carry standing passenger?

80km/h.

What is the maximum permitted speed on a **motorway** of a **single-decker** bus or minibus (having passenger accommodation for more than 8 persons) and which is designed to carry standing passengers?

65km/h.

What is the maximum permitted speed on a **dual carriageway** of a **single-decker** bus or minibus (having passenger accommodation for more than 8 persons) which **is** designed to carry standing passengers?

65km/h.

What is the maximum permitted speed on a **national primary road** of a **single-decker** bus or minibus having passenger accommodation for more than 8 persons and which **is** designed to carry standing passengers?

65km/h.

What is the maximum permitted speed limit on a **motorway** of a **double-decker** bus or minibus (having passenger accommodation for more than 8 persons) and which **is** designed to carry standing passengers?

65km/h.

What is the maximum permitted speed on a **dual carriageway** of a **double-decker** bus or minibus (having passenger accommodation for more than 8 persons) and which **is** designed to carry standing passengers?

65km/h.

What is the maximum permitted speed on a **national primary road** of a **double-decker** bus or minibus (having passenger accommodation for more than 8 persons) and which **is** designed to carry standing passengers?

65km/h.

Type of road	Not designed for standing passengers	Designed for standing passengers
All buses are subject to the following speed limits, unless a lower speed limit is in place.		
Motorways	100km/h	65km/h
Dual carriageways	100km/h	65km/h
National roads	80km/h	65km/h

Vehicle dimensions

There are a number of regulations relating to the size of a bus, and as a bus driver, you are expected to know the maximum size allowed and, just as important, the actual height and width of the bus you are driving.

What is the maximum width of a bus?

2.55 metres.

> You should always know the width of your vehicle, and bear it in mind when driving beside parked vehicles or on narrow roads. The maximum permitted width of a bus is 2.55 metres.

What is the maximum height of a double-decker bus?

4.57 metres.

> You should always know the height of your vehicle, and bear it in mind when driving in areas with restricted heights, such as low and arch bridges, and bus garage doors. A collision could result in serious or fatal injury to passengers. The maximum permitted height is 4.57 metres.

Braking and speed limiters

Certain buses are required to have a speed limiter installed. The questions in this section test your knowledge of this issue.

What buses are required to have a speed limiter fitted?

Buses with more than 8 passengers seats.

What is the maximum speed limiter setting for buses that are not designed to carry standing passengers?

100km/h.

> A speed limiter is a device that sets a maximum to the speed at which a vehicle can be driven. Buses that have more than 8 passengers seats and that are not designed to carry standing passengers must be fitted with a speed limiter set to a maximum of 100km/h. If they are designed to carry standing passengers, the speed limiter must be set to 65km/h.

Crosswinds and vehicle safety

What effect can strong crosswinds have on a double-decker bus?

It makes it more liable to turn over.

A double-decker bus can be blown off course or even blown over by cross-winds. When driving a bus, you should be aware of these potential dangers especially in open areas and on motorways. Areas where strong cross-winds are likely to occur are generally identified by a warning sign (wind sock).

Carrying passengers

The questions in this section check that you know the regulations relating to the number of passengers that you can carry in a bus or minibus, and that you know how to drive and operate the bus in a way that ensures the comfort and safety of the passengers.

How many passengers may be carried on a bus?

As many as the vehicle's PSV plate specifies.

The maximum number of passengers that may be carried on a bus is specified on the PSV plate. This has implications for the speed limits that apply to the vehicle.

What is the maximum number of adult passengers that a driver who holds a D1 licence may carry in a minibus?

16 passengers.

If you hold a D1 driving licence, you are allowed to drive a bus or coach with a maximum of 16 passenger seats.

What is a bus driver's main responsibility?

The safety and comfort of the passengers.

If you drive a bus, your main responsibility is to ensure the safety and comfort of your passengers. This means delivering them safely to their destination, on time, in a courteous and efficient manner.

What should a driver check before moving off after dropping off passengers?

Both exterior mirrors.

Before moving off, check your off-side exterior mirror for overtaking traffic and other road users and your nearside exterior mirror for intending passengers rushing to catch the bus. Check these mirrors as many times as necessary.

What effect could overloading with passengers or goods have on a bus?

It can impair the bus's road-holding ability.

Overloading your vehicle can adversely affect the road-holding capabilities of the vehicle. As a bus driver, you are responsible for the safety and comfort of your passengers, and overloading the vehicle puts them at risk.

In what circumstances should the emergency doors be locked when children are being carried on a bus?

Never – easy entry and exit from a bus or minibus is essential for safety.

For safety and legal reasons, emergency doors and exits should never be locked when a bus or coach is in service.

What should a driver do to ensure the safety and comfort of their passengers?

Drive smoothly and brake evenly.

Read the road ahead and plan well in advance for braking and stopping and for changes in direction. This style of driving will help to ensure that your passengers arrive safely at their destinations.

When driving a double-decker bus, how would a driver monitor the passengers on the top deck?

Frequent use of the internal mirrors and cameras if fitted.

Whilst driving a double-decker bus, what are the interior mirrors used for?

Observing passengers who may be standing.

Most double-decker buses are fitted with cameras or interior mirrors that are positioned so as to enable the driver to check exits and entrances, stairs and the top deck.

Why should a driver accelerate smoothly?

To improve passenger comfort.

To reduce wear on the engine.

To improve fuel consumption.

To reduce wear on the tyres

What effect should driving smoothly have?

It should preserve the condition of the bus, thus reducing maintenance costs.

Your main responsibility as a bus driver is to ensure the safety and comfort of your passengers.

Read the road ahead and plan well in advance for accelerating, for braking and stopping, and for changes in direction. This style of driving will help to ensure that your passengers arrive safely at their destinations. It will also reduce the environmental impact of the vehicle, enhance fuel efficiency and reduce wear and tear on the engine and tyres.

When letting passengers off the bus, what should a driver do to ensure their safety?

Let the passengers off only when the bus is stopped close to the kerb at a bus stop.

Before opening the doors to let passengers off, make sure that they can alight safely, by checking for other road users, such as pedestrians or cyclists, that may be coming up on the inside.

What driving behaviour could result in passengers getting thrown about?

Cornering harshly.

Braking severely.

Read the road ahead and plan well in advance for braking and stopping and for changes in direction. This style of driving will help to ensure that you brake smoothly and turn at a speed that does not inconvenience or endanger your passengers.

How should a driver show care to the passengers?

By allowing them time to get seated.

By not exceeding the permitted number of passengers.

Treat your passengers with care and respect. When you pick up passengers, make sure that they are seated before moving off, and drive in such a way that they are not inconvenienced or endangered. Do not carry more passengers than the vehicle is designed for.

When may a driver carry a passenger on the trailer of a bus?

It is never permitted.

Passengers must never be carried in the trailer. If you drive a bus, you are responsible for the safety and comfort of your passengers, and for the vehicle itself. You need to take particular care when towing a trailer, especially when reversing.

Where should passengers' heavy luggage be stored?

In the luggage compartment.

As a bus driver, you are responsible for the safety and comfort of your passengers, and for the vehicle itself. Store heavy luggage in the luggage compartment – if it is in the passenger compartment, it could pose a danger to the passengers in the event of sudden deceleration or change in direction.

Safety equipment

What safety equipment must be carried on a bus or minibus?

A fire extinguisher and first aid kit.

All buses or minibuses must carry an advance warning triangle, a fire extinguisher and a first-aid kit. These are the basic essentials that may be needed in an emergency situation, such as a collision.

Getting out of the vehicle

In most buses, the driver's seat is considerably higher than in a car. Getting into and out of the cab involves climbing up or down, and it is important that you do so safely. Before you get out, check that opening the door will not interfere with other road users, and that you can get down safely.

Similarly, when you are letting passengers off the bus, you must make sure that they can do so safely.

How should a driver exit the cab of a bus with the driver's door on the offside?

By climbing down while facing inwards.

When getting out of the cab of a bus that has the driver's door on the off-side, face inwards, so that you can climb down safely in a gradual manner.

When should the passenger door be opened on a bus or minibus?

When stopped at a place where it is safe for passengers to get out.

You should allow passengers to get on and off the bus only when it is stopped in a safe place. This (apart from emergencies) is the only situation in which the passenger door should be opened.

When leaving the cab of a bus, what should a driver ensure?

That the parking brake is on.

That the electrical master switch is off.

That the engine is switched off.

What should the driver check before leaving the cab of a bus?

That it is safe to disembark and that no other vehicles pose a potential hazard for the driver or the passengers leaving the bus.

When parking a bus, you should make sure that it is in a safe place, the parking brake is on, the engine is switched off, and the electrical master switch is off. Before leaving the cab, check for approaching traffic to make sure it is safe to disembark.

When children are alighting from a school bus, what advice should a driver give them?

To stay well in off the road until the bus has moved away.

Schoolchildren in particular can be excitable, unruly and unpredictable. When passengers are getting off the bus, advise them to stay off the road until the bus has moved away, and check that the road is clear behind and to the sides before moving off.

What should a driver do when wishing to stop to allow passengers to get off the bus?

Stop where the passengers getting off the bus will not be in danger from other traffic.

You should allow passengers to get on and off the bus only when it is stopped in a safe place where they will not be in danger from other traffic or in a position where their footing may be undermined.

In relation to the passenger doors, what in particular should a driver be aware of when driving a bus?

That the passenger doors should never be locked.

In relation to the emergency doors, what in particular should a driver be aware of when driving a bus?

That the emergency doors should never be locked.

> For safety and legal reasons, emergency doors and exits should never be locked when a bus or coach is in service.

Collisions and breakdowns

If your bus is involved in a collision or if it breaks down, your first priority should be to ensure the safety of your passengers. The questions in this section check that you know how to act in such an event.

What should a driver do when involved in a collision where nobody is injured but where fuel has spilt onto the road?

Get the passengers to a safe area as quickly as possible.

> If you are involved in a collision where fuel has been spilt, you should get the passengers off the bus and to a safe place as soon as possible, and not allow them back on the bus until the emergency services have taken charge of the situation.

What should a driver do if the bus is broken down in the middle of the road following a collision in which nobody is injured?

Guide each passenger individually to the roadside.
Guide the passengers to safety.

> If you are involved in a collision, you should get the passengers off the bus and escort them (individually if necessary) to a safe place, and not allow them back on the bus until the emergency services have taken charge of the situation.

A bus or coach is involved in a collision on a motorway. What should the driver do?

Move the bus to the hard shoulder and evacuate the passengers behind the crash barrier.

If you are involved in a collision on a motorway, move the bus to the hard shoulder if possible and safely evacuate the passengers behind the crash barriers and up the embankment, as the hard shoulder is the most dangerous place on a motorway. Do not allow the passengers back on the bus until the emergency services have taken charge of the situation.

What should a driver do first if the bus or minibus breaks down on an automatic level crossing?

Guide the passengers to safety as quickly as possible and use the phone at the level crossing to alert Iarnród Éireann of the danger.

If your bus breaks down on a level crossing, get the passengers off the bus and to a safe place without delay and phone the signal operator so that trains can be stopped.

When should a driver use hazard warning lights?

When the vehicle has broken down.

To warn following traffic of an unexpected hazard ahead.

You generally use the hazard warning lights to warn other road users of an unexpected hazard ahead or to signal that your vehicle has broken down and is causing an obstruction.

Using the mirrors

What should a driver check for in the left-hand side mirror?

For vehicles coming up on the left.

Mirrors help you to monitor road and traffic conditions to the sides and rear of your vehicle, so that you can make better decisions. The left-hand side mirror is particularly useful for seeing road users coming up on your inside when you are changing direction or in slow-moving traffic. It is also useful for checking for intending passengers before moving off.

As a bus driver, you must know how to use your mirrors effectively to monitor road and traffic conditions to the sides and rear of your vehicle.

Turning into a minor road

In this situation, what should a driver do when entering the minor road?

Take adequate space on the approach
to avoid mounting the kerb.

When turning left into a minor road with a bus or coach, you may have to adopt a position on the road to the right of your normal position. This can lead other road users to believe that you intend turning right. Check carefully all around your vehicle, signal your intentions and take up position far enough to the right so that you can turn left without mounting the near-side kerb.

Driving through a bus station

When you are driving through a bus station or other confined space, you need to be on the look-out for pedestrians and other vehicles. The questions in this section check that you understand your responsibilities in this respect.

What should a driver do when driving through a bus station?

Watch out for people leaving or boarding other buses.

What should a driver do when driving through a bus station?

Drive at a slow speed.

When driving in confined spaces such as bus garages and bus stations, you should take extra care and drive at slower speeds, as passengers, garage staff and other pedestrians may be walking in the area, or alighting from or boarding other buses.

Suspension systems

There are two basic types of suspension systems used on buses: air suspension and leaf-spring suspension. The questions in this section check that you know the advantages and disadvantages associated with each type.

What effect does an air suspension system have on a bus?

A comfortable journey for passengers.

Most buses are fitted with air suspension. This improves passenger comfort and reduces wear and tear on vehicles, tyres and road surfaces.

Compared to air suspension, what effect does spring leaf suspension have on a bus?

A less comfortable journey for passengers.

Most buses today are fitted with air suspension. This improves passenger comfort and reduces wear and tear on vehicles, tyres and road surfaces. Spring-leaf suspension is an older type of suspension which is less effective in these respects.

Motorway driving

When can the hard shoulder of a motorway be used?

When stopping in an emergency.

If you are driving on a motorway and your vehicle develops a problem, you should leave the motorway immediately if possible. If it is not possible, pull in and stop on the hard shoulder as far as possible to the left, and contact the emergency services without delay.

Moving off

When you are driving a bus, you need to take extra care when you are moving off, because sudden movement can unbalance any passengers who are standing, and also because there may be people who are still trying to get on or off the bus.

What should a driver be aware of before moving off?

The effect of any sudden movement of the bus on passengers.

Persons attempting to get off the bus.

What should a driver be aware of before moving off from a bus stop?

Persons attempting to get on the bus.

Before moving off, braking, stopping or turning, remember that any sudden movement of the vehicle can cause discomfort or danger to passengers, particularly any that are standing or moving around the vehicle. Before moving off from a bus stop, check the appropriate mirrors to make sure that there is nobody attempting to get on or off.

Notes

Notes

Notes

Notes

Notes

Notes

Notes

Notes

Notes

Notes

Notes

Notes

Notes

Notes